Problem Solving and Comprehension

Sixth Edition

Arthur Whimbey
Text Reconstruction Across the Curriculum Institute
Albuquerque, New Mexico

Jack Lochhead
DeLiberate Thinking
Conway, Massachusetts

LAWRENCE ERLBAUM ASSOCIATES, PUBLISHERS
1999   Mahwah, New Jersey   London

Lawrence Erlbaum Associates, Inc., Publishers
10 Industrial Avenue
Mahwah, NJ 07430

Cover design by Kathryn Houghtaling Lacey

Library of Congress Cataloging-in-Publication Data

Whimbey, Arthur.
Problem solving and comprehension / Arthur Whimbey, Jack
    Lochhead. — 6th ed.
    p. cm.
ISBN 0-8058-3274-2 (pbk.)
1. Problem solving—Problems, exercises, etc. 2. Comprehen-
    sion—Problems, exercises, etc. 3. Reasoning—Problems,
    exercises, etc. I. Lochhead, Jack, 1944–   .
  BF449.W45 1999
  153.4'3—dc21
                                            98-33156
                                               CIP

Books published by Lawrence Erlbaum Associates are printed
on acid-free paper, and their bindings are chosen for strength
and durability.

Printed in the United States of America
10 9 8 7 6 5 4 3 2 1

Problem Solving
and
Comprehension

Sixth Edition

CONTENTS

PREFACE

Suppose you asked people the following questions: Would you like greater skill in solving math and logic problems? Would you like to sharpen your grasp of the ideas you read in scientific publications, medical reports, textbooks, and legal contracts?

Most people would answer "yes" to these questions. They'd be happy to gain increased capability to reason—because in today's world it's almost impossible to avoid doing some problem solving and technical reading.

The business world and the classroom have always put a premium on mental skills. Today, even in the home, checkbooks and budgets need balancing, wits are challenged by directions for assembling toys and stereo or computer equipment, income tax forms must be deciphered, and so on.

This book shows you how to increase your power to analyze problems and comprehend what you read and hear. First it outlines and illustrates the methods that good problem solvers use in attacking complex ideas. Then it gives you practice in applying these methods to a variety of questions in comprehension and reasoning. As you work through the book you will witness a steady improvement in your analytical thinking skills. You will develop confidence in your own ability to solve problems, and this increased confidence will give you a vigorous, positive attitude when attacking problems. If you're willing to work and practice, you will be rewarded.

For example, at some time you may have to take a test to enter college, medical school, or law school—or to be hired for a particular job. Here are some of the tests commonly used for college and job selection:

- Scholastic Aptitude Test (SAT)
- Graduate Record Examination (GRE)
- ACT Work Keys
- Terra Nova
- Law School Admission Test (LSAT)
- Wonderlic Personnel Test
- United States Employment Service General Aptitude Test Battery
- Civil Service Examinations

Tests such as these are made up of problems; the better you are at problem solving, the higher your scores will be. If you put the techniques you learn in this book to work, you can expect to see real gains in your scores on selection tests.

Your school grades can also be improved with the techniques you learn here because you will have a two-edged sword. First, you'll be better prepared to understand your textbooks and lectures so that your mastery of courses will be fuller and deeper. You'll be a better thinker and learner. In addition, when exam time rolls around, your sharpened reading and reasoning skills will give you a strong advantage in interpreting questions and answering them.

The thinking skills you learn in this book go beyond tests and school learning. You'll find them useful in all occupations that involve reading technical materials or tackling difficult problems. With the growth of technology, such occupations represent an expanding portion of the job market. X-ray technicians, TV repairpersons, registered nurses, computer programmers, and accountants are all called upon to comprehend and coordinate advanced areas of knowledge. Automobile repair has become a field of specialists. Modern fuel injection systems are so intricate that a person can't understand and repair them without the ability to read complex descriptions and directions. Skilled operators are needed for the new automotive diagnostic equipment, which is used to get a profile of engine performance and difficulties. Even farming today has become a detailed science in which soils are chemically analyzed and then treated with spectrums of additives to produce maximum yields of high-paying crops. To be successful, a farmer has to have considerable knowledge about both chemical products and crop-market trends.

In short, the techniques you learn in this book can help you on tests, in your academic courses, and in any occupations that involve analyzing, untangling, or comprehending knotty ideas.

NEW IN THE SIXTH EDITION

After 20 years any book will become a little dated. Yet much of *Problem Solving and Comprehension* is as fresh and as useful today as it was when the first edition was published in 1979. Strong analytical thinking is a constant. It changes little over the centuries.

In preparing the sixth edition of this book we made some minor changes to the language: We changed the names of some of our characters to make them represent more accurately the cross section of students attending today's schools; we changed the dates in some problems; we updated the technology referred to in others.

By far the biggest change of the past 20 years occurs not in this book but in the educational system in which it is used. We have added a chapter to describe these changes and to show how the techniques taught in *Problem Solving and Comprehension* relate to the new educational standards and tests. Twenty years ago many of the tests and state curriculum standards placed little emphasis on analytical thinking skills. Today these skills are at the heart of all sound educational designs. The need for a strong course in analytical reasoning is far greater today than ever before. We hope, therefore, that this revised book will serve the citizens of the 21st century as well as it has their parents.

—*Arthur Whimbey*
—*Jack Lochhead*

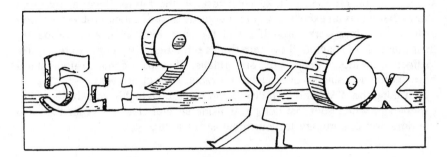

I. TEST YOUR MIND—SEE HOW IT WORKS

A good way to begin a thinking skills program is to take stock of your own thinking habits and compare them to those of other people. On page 3 you'll find a test called the Whimbey Analytical Skills Inventory (WASI). The WASI is the type of test you might take in applying for a job or college program. If you are using this book in a class, your instructor will ask you to take the WASI and make an extra copy of your answers. Then he will collect one copy.

Here is how the WASI differs from other tests. Usually when you take such tests you don't get a chance to discuss your answers. Sometimes you don't even find out what your scores are. But with the WASI you will spend several days in class debriefing—going over the test item by item. For each question, your instructor will call on different students to explain how they handled it. In that way, students can compare their problem-solving strategies. Furthermore, if students answered questions incorrectly when they took the test, the instructor may ask them to explain the method they employed that led to the wrong answer. Pay special attention to these explanations of errors, since they will show you how *not* to deal with such problems. Learning to recognize and avoid ineffective problem-solving methods is an important part of the training. Also notice the sequences of thoughts used by students who answered the question successfully. Compare the approaches leading to the correct answer with those leading to incorrect answers. Pinpoint how the approaches differ. Most importantly, for every question that you answer incorrectly, be sure you understand exactly why the error occurred, and how you can avoid such an error in the future.

If you are not using this book in a class, have a brother, sister, parent or some other friend take the WASI and then compare your answers and strategies.

Asking people to explain their answers to the test questions, and then to compare the explanations with those of others, accomplishes two things. First, it takes the mystery out of mental tests, making them less threatening

1

should you be required to take such tests in the future. Second, research shows that this is an excellent way for people to improve their problem-solving skills. When they work through a test together, explaining and comparing their methods of solution, they learn from each other. They come to recognize ineffective methods, dead ends, and pitfalls. They also come to understand how to attack problems effectively and reach correct answers.

Taking the WASI and then discussing it can be a highly valuable learning experience. When your instructor sets aside several class hours for this, use the time and opportunity to your greatest advantage.

WASI TEST
WHIMBEY ANALYTICAL SKILLS INVENTORY

Instructions

This inventory consists of 38 questions. Some of the questions are multiple choice, while others are more complex. For each of the multiple choice questions, circle the answer which you think is correct.

Here are two sample questions. Please try to answer them.

1. If you started with $25.00 and then spent $3.00 to go to a movie, how much would you have left?

    a. $23.00   *b.* $22.00   *c.* $21.00   *d.* $12.00

2. Circle the fifth word in this sentence.

For the first sample question you should have circled alternative *b.*, since $22.00 are left after spending $3.00 for the movie. With the second question you should have circled the word "in," because it is the fifth word in the sentence.

If you have any questions, please ask your instructor to answer them. Otherwise, wait until your instructor asks you to turn the page, then begin.

1. Which word is different from the other 3 words?

    a. yell   *b.* talk   *c.* pencil   *d.* whisper

2. Which letter is as far away from *K* in the alphabet as *J* is from *G*?

    a. K   *b. M*   *c. N*   *d. G*   *e. I*

3. If you are facing east and turn left, then make an about-face and turn left again, in which direction are you facing?

    a. east   *b.* north   *c.* west   *d.* south   *e.* southwest

4. Which pair of words fits best in the blanks?

    Arm is to wrist as _____ is to _____.

    a. leg: foot   *b.* thigh: ankle   *c.* leg: ankle   *d.* leg: knee

5. 20 is related to 30 as 10 is related to _____?

    a. 5   *b.* 25   *c.* 60   *d.* 15   *e.* 10

6. Which set of letters is different from the other 3 sets?

    a. EFGE   *b. BCDB*   *c. KLML*   *d. OPQO*

7. In a different language *liro cas* means "red tomato," *dum cas dan* means "big red barn" and *xer dan* means "big horse." What is the word for *barn* in this language?

    a. dum   *b. liro*   *c. cas*   *d. dan*   *e. xer*

8. Write the 2 letters which should appear next in the series.

$$C\ B\ F\ E\ I\ H\ L\ K \underline{\hspace{1cm}} \underline{\hspace{1cm}}$$

9. There are 3 separate, equal-size boxes, and inside each box there are 2 separate small boxes, and inside each of the small boxes there are 4 even smaller boxes. How many boxes are there altogether?

   a. 24   *b.* 13   *c.* 21   *d.* 33   *e.* some other number

10. Ten full crates of walnuts weigh 410 lb, while an empty crate weighs 10 lb. How much do the walnuts alone weigh?

   a. 400 lb   *b.* 390 lb   *c.* 310 lb   *d.* 320 lb   *e.* 420 lb

11. One number in the series below is incorrect. What should that number be?

$$3\quad 4\quad 6\quad 9\quad 13\quad 18\quad 24\quad 33$$

   a. 33   *b.* 7   *c.* 24   *c.* 31   *e.* 32

12. The first figure is related to the second figure in the same way that the third figure is related to one of the answer choices. Pick the answer.

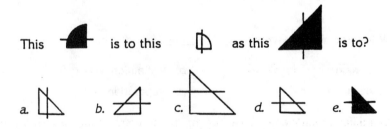

13. Which pair of words best fits the meaning of the sentence?

   _____ the dog was big, he was _____ heavy.

   a. Since—not   *b.* Although—very
   c. Although—not   *d.* Because—nevertheless

14. Write the 2 numbers which should appear next in the series.

    3   9   5   15   11   33   29   ____   ____

15. An orthopedist is a _____ specialist.

    a. brain   *b.* heart   *c.* ear and throat   *d.* lung   *e.* bone

16. An equivocal statement is _____.

    a. relevant   *b.* equivalent
    c. credible   *d.* somewhat loud
    e. ambiguous

17. Three empty cereal boxes weigh 9 ozs and each box holds 11 ozs of cereal. How much do 2 full boxes of cereal weigh together?

    a. 20 ozs   *b.* 40 ozs   *c.* 14 ozs   *d.* 28 ozs   *e.* 15 ozs

18. Cross out the letter after the letter in the word **pardon** which is in the same position in the word as it is in the alphabet.

19. A journey always involves a _____?

    a. person   *b.* destination
    c. distance   *d.* preparation

20. In how many days of the week does the third letter of the day's name immediately follow the first letter of the day's name in the alphabet?

    a. 1   *b.* 2   *c.* 3   *d.* 4   *e.* 5

21. Which pair of words is different from the other 3 pairs?

a. walk—slowly

b. speak—loud

c. read—book

d. lift—quickly

22. The top 4 figures form a series which changes in a systematic manner according to some rule. Try to discover the rule and choose from among the alternatives the figure which should occur next in the series.

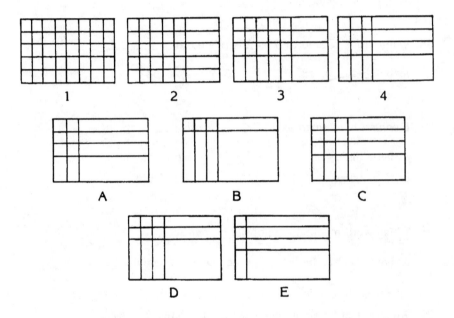

23. Which number is repeated first in the following series?

5 9 4 8 2 3 6 1 7 4 7 6 7 8 9 1 5 2 3 5 8 9 5 3 5 4 3 7 1

a. 7   b. 8   c. 6   d. 4   e. 5

24. Which pair of words fits best in the blanks?

    Oven is to *bake* as _____ is to _____.

    a. automobile: carry   b. dishwasher: dishes
    c. food: ice   d. vacuum cleaner: rug

25. Write the 3 letters which should come next in this series.

    B A A C E E D I I E M M F ____ ____ ____

26. *One third* is related to *9* as *2* is related to _____.

    a. 6   b. 18   c. 36   d. 54   e. 99

27. *Elephant* is to *small* as _____ is to _____.

    a. large: little   b. hippopotamus: mouse

    c. turtle: slow   d. lion: timid

28. Which word means the opposite of *demise*?

    a. hasty   b. birth   c. accept   d. embrace

29. Which set of letters is different from the other 3 sets?

    a. *HRTG*   b. *NOMP*   c. *XACW*   d. *LDFK*

30. *Hospital* is to *sickness* as _____ is to _____.

    a. patient: disease   b. jail: prisoner

    c. doctor: patient   d. school: ignorance

    e. nurse: illness

31. A train travels 50 mi while a car travels 40 mi. How many miles will the train travel while the car travels 60 mi?

    a. 60   *b.* 50   *c.* 70   *d.* 75   *e.* 80

32. *Heretic* is to *religious* as _____ is to _____.

    a. disbelief: faith   b. adversary: cooperative

    c. sinner: punishment   d. disrespectful: pious

33. How many sixths are in 12/2?

    a. 6   *b.* 1   *c.* 36   *d.* 4   *e.* 24

34. 2, 9, 3, 5, 1, 8, 4. Take the difference between the second number and the next-to-last number, then add it to the fourth number. If this sum is less than 6, write the word "go" in this space _____; otherwise, write the word "stop" in this space _____.

35. Which word is different from the other 3 words?

    a. peregrination   *b.* pilgrimage

    c. outlandish   *d.* promenade

36. 3, 6, 4, 2, 5, 9, 1. Add the second number to the sixth number, then divide by 3 and write the quotient, unless it is greater than 5; in this case add the first number to the next-to-last number and divide by 4. What is your final answer?

    a. 3   *b.* 5   *c.* 2   *d.* 4   *e.* some other number

37. Select the answer which is most nearly equivalent in meaning to the following statement.

> Show me the man you honor. I know by that symptom, better than any other, what you are yourself.
>
> —Carlyle

a. The works of great scholars should be read and studied.

b. A man can be judged by his works.

c. A man can be judged by those he emulates.

d. Each human being has his own unique worth.

38. *Optimist* is to *pessimist* as _____ is to _____.

a. solace: morose   b. sanguine: morose

c. benefactor: patron   d. eulogy: gloomy

END.   When you are finished, check back over your work.

II. ERRORS IN REASONING

One way to improve your analytical skills is to see the types of errors that people frequently make in solving problems, and then guard against making those same errors yourself.

Various types of errors undoubtedly came to light in your discussion of the WASI. This chapter analyzes a sample of errors made by students in courses that we have taught. Read through these errors and see how they compare to the ones you made.

Occasionally errors are made on the WASI because people don't have enough information to answer a question. For example, on vocabulary questions (such as question # 15) a person might not know the meaning of the words. But most errors are not of this type. Instead, people have sufficient facts yet miss questions because their analyses and reasoning processes break down. Here are four ways in which the breakdowns frequently occur:

1. Person fails to observe and use all the relevant facts of a problem.

2. Person fails to approach the problem in a systematic step-by-step manner, making leaps in logic and jumping to conclusions without checking them.

3. Person fails to spell out relationships fully.

4. Person is sloppy and inaccurate in collecting information and carrying out mental activities.

These sources of error tend to be interrelated; however, one may be more prominent than the others with some particular person or problem. Examples of all four sources of error follow.

Error Analysis of Sample IQ Questions

In this section we will review errors made on the following questions from the WASI: Questions 7, 9, 10, 12, 18, 22, 27 and 28. These questions are representative of the types of problems that are found on most IQ tests. Let's begin with question 7.

Question 7

In a different language *liro cas* means "red tomato," *dum cas dan* means "big red barn" and *xer dan* means "big horse." What is the word for *barn* in this language?

   a. dum   *b. liro*   *c. cas*   *d. dan*   *e. xer*

This is a fairly easy question, but one which is often missed by nonanalytical thinkers. The most common error is to say that *dan* means barn because *dan* and barn both occupy the third position in "*dum cas dan*" and "big red barn." The error fails to take into account that "*xer dan*" means "big horse." It is an example of the one-shot thinking and lack of concern for total accuracy which researchers have observed to be characteristic of nonanalytical thinkers.

Question 9

There are 3 separate, equal-size boxes, and inside each box there are 2 separate small boxes, and inside each of the small boxes there are 4 even smaller boxes. How many boxes are there altogether?

   a. 24   *b.* 13   *c.* 21   *d.* 33   *e.* some other number

This question is especially interesting because its solution is quite straightforward, yet it is often missed. It illustrates the lack of skill which some people have in spelling out ideas fully and accurately.

The simplest way to solve this problem is to draw a diagram representing correctly the relationship of the boxes.

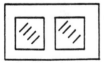  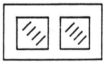

A student who chose answer *b* described her inadequate reasoning as follows:

> I pictured the three boxes and the two smaller boxes inside the three boxes . . . I added three plus two (which gave five) and counted the four other boxes twice. Five plus eight gave me 13.

This student didn't spell the diagram out fully. Instead she went ahead and added numbers without carefully considering exactly which numbers should be added and why.

Many people approach mathematics problems in this way. They perform inappropriate numerical operations because they don't clarify in their own minds the exact relationship of the facts in the problem.

Question 10
Ten full crates of walnuts weigh 410 lb, while an empty crate weighs 10 lb. How much do the walnuts alone weigh?

a. 400 lb   b. 390 lb   c. 310 lb   d. 320 lb   e. 420 lb

This is a conventional math word problem, something which frightens a large percentage of students and adults. They feel that a special inborn ability is required for mathematics, an ability in which they rate a great big zero.

When you look at this problem closely, you see that it doesn't require any mysterious ability. All that this problem demands is that the facts be spelled out fully and accurately. Once that is done, the remaining arithmetic is simple.

Here is a diagram which spells the facts out fully. It shows that the total weight is composed of 11 parts, the weight of the 10 crates and the weight of the walnuts.

Total Weight: 410 Pounds

10 lb	10 lb	10 lb	10 lb	10 lb	10 lb	10 lb	10 lb	10 lb	10 lb

Walnut Weight: 310 pounds

You may not have actually visualized this diagram in working the problem, but conceptually you used a similar model. You had to sort the total weight into the various parts shown in the diagram in order to compute the answer.

Students who have trouble with this and other math problems haven't learned to spell numerical relationships out fully so that correct calculations can be made. For example, a mistake frequently made with this problem is to answer 400 pounds, showing that the person did not take all 10 boxes into account.

A revealing answer to this problem is alternative *e*, which is 420 pounds. This answer is sometimes selected, even though it doesn't make sense. The walnuts alone can't possibly weigh more than the walnuts plus the crates. This answer shows how anxious and flustered some people get in doing math. They see two numbers in the problem, 410 and 10, and immediately add. They read math problems with less care and patient thought than they would the inscriptions on tombstones of strangers in a dark, frightening cemetery. They feel conquered by math, and so they never even begin calling their analytical skills out to battle.

Question 12

The first figure is related to the second figure in the same way that the third figure is related to one of the answer choices. Pick the answer.

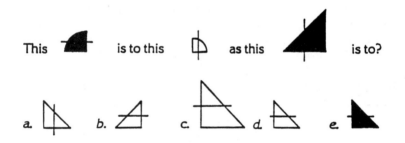

This is a fairly easy figural problem. Still, people make errors because they are inaccurate in observing or using the given information in understanding the analogy and selecting an answer. For example, they may neglect to change the shading and choose answer *e*. Or they may neglect size and choose *c*.

Question 18

Cross out the letter after the letter in the word **pardon** which is in the same position in the word as it is in the alphabet.

This is a fairly difficult verbal reasoning problem. One interesting thing about it is that while on the surface it appears to be very different from question 12 (above), errors on the two questions come about for the very same reasons. People fail to search out and use all the available information.

One frequent error is to cross out the *d* in *pardon*, rather than crossing the letter after the *d*. The person making this error has lost part of the problem.

Another less frequent error is to cross out the *d* in *word*, as shown below.

Cross out the letter after the letter in the word pardon which is in the same position in the worɗ as it is in the alphabet.

People who make this error haven't learned to work step-by-step through a complex sentence. They don't think through the sentence in the following way:

Cross out the letter after the letter (so I have to cross out a letter) in the word (cross out a letter in some word) pardon (so pardon must be the word).

Question 22
The top four figures form a series which changes in a systematic manner according to some rule. Try to discover the rule and choose from among the alternatives the figure which should occur next in the series.

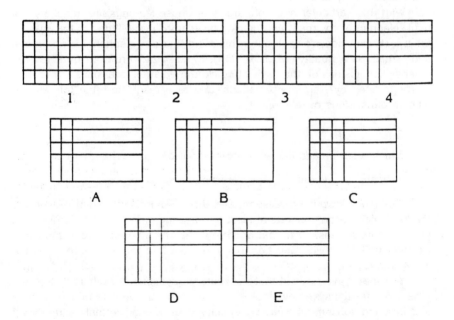

Here is another problem which is missed frequently although it involves no obscure or esoteric ideas. Errors arise from inaccuracies in making observations and building them into a system or rule which leads to the answer. For example, a student who chose answer *e* explained his thinking as follows:

> I noticed that first there are some lines taken away. Then there are more lines taken away going the other way. Then there are more lines taken away going up and down. So I guess the answer should take more lines away. I guess answer *e*.

I asked him whether he had counted the lines to see exactly how many were deleted in each figure and he answered that he had not, as it seemed too confusing. As you see, this student had never learned to accurately keep track of facts in problem solving.

Question 27

Elephant is to *small* _____ as is to _____.

a. large: little   b. hippopotamus: mouse

c. turtle: slow   d. lion: timid

Verbal analogies like this one play a large role on tests such as the SAT, GRE, and various other aptitude tests and IQ measures. Analogy questions are widely used because they tap a person's ability to define ideas and relationships fully and accurately.

With this particular question, students whose leanings are nonanalytical read "elephant is to small" and quickly decide on "large: little" as the answer. Such a student doesn't spell out in his mind that an "elephant" is an animal and "small" is a quality, whereas "large" and "little" are both qualities. He reaches conclusions on the basis of quick immediate impressions rather than thorough, step-by-step interpretations, and as a result he often misses significant dimensions of relationships.

Question 28

Which word means the opposite of *demise?*

a. hasty   b. birth   c. accept   d. embrace

This is a vocabulary question, and there is hardly a mental test on the market which doesn't include at least a few of them. In this question you are given a word and asked to find another word which is opposite in meaning. At other times (as with question 16) you must find the word that is similar in meaning.

You may have noticed that vocabulary questions are different than the other test questions we have looked at. Most test questions require reasoning and problem solving, whereas vocabulary questions are mainly a matter of recall.

This apparent disparity is cleared up when you consider how vocabulary is acquired. A rich vocabulary is the by-product of careful thinking in verbal communication. People who think analytically listen and read for complete understanding of relevant ideas. When they encounter a new word they try to estimate its meaning from the context. If they are still uncertain, they take out the dictionary and study the various entries, interpreting and contrasting ideas and terms until they are sure of the word's definition. In short, although vocabulary questions do not require problem solving at the time one takes a test, these questions do reflect the precise thinking that people employ in acquiring vocabulary.

Summary

In this chapter we have looked at the types of test questions that are used to measure reasoning ability, and have seen that errors are primarily caused by a lack of accuracy and thoroughness in thinking. Research has shown that accuracy and thoroughness are mental habits which can be cultivated through training and exercise. This book provides some of that training. But you need to go further on your own. With everything you read, practice carefulness in comprehending ideas and relationships. And in solving problems, continually check yourself for accuracy and completeness. Initially this may be difficult and require conscious discipline, just as learning good typing habits or correct swimming movements may at first be difficult. Gradually, however, the attitudes and skills of tight reasoning will become as natural to you as swimming, skating, driving, typing, or any of the various other skills that you have learned with practice and time.

Although accuracy and thoroughness are beneficial to every kind of activity in which we engage, you are likely to be more accurate in some areas than in others. It is a good idea to identify the areas in which you are least accurate and to make special efforts to practice problems in those areas. Errors on the WASI problems (13, 15, 16, 28, 32, 35, 37, 38) suggest a need to practice Verbal Reasoning problems, pages 41–135. You may also need to develop your English vocabulary, which can be done by increasing the amount of reading you do, and by making sure to look up the words you do not know or of which you are unsure. You might also work through a vocabulary development text such as chapter 34 in Linden and Whimbey (1990a). Errors on the WASI problems (9, 10, 17, 18, 20, 22, 23, 34, 36) indicate you need practice on following sequential instructions, problems 32–43 on pages 133–135 and chapter 10 on pages 221–238. Errors on WASI problems (2, 3, 4, 5, 12, 24, 26, 30) indicate you need practice forming Analogies, pages 141–192. Errors on WASI problems (1, 6, 19) can be traced to the specific area of Writing Relationship Sentences, pages 155–169. Errors on WASI problems (8, 11, 14, 21, 25, 29) relate to the Analysis of Trends and Patterns, pages 193–219. Errors on WASI problems 31 and 33 suggest a need to practice Solving Mathematical Word Problems, pages 239–331. But the most important practice is the practice of being thorough and accurate with any kind of problem. The following Checklist provides an introductory guide to pitfalls the thorough problem solver must be careful to avoid.

CHECKLIST OF ERRORS IN PROBLEM SOLVING

Following is a checklist of sources and types of errors in problem solving. Some of the items overlap, referring to different aspects of the same fault in working problems, but this overlap is unavoidable because the various factors that underlie problem-solving skill are interrelated. Read the checklist aloud, discussing any items that are unclear. Then, as you solve problems, be careful not to make these errors. If you recognize some particular error to which you are especially prone, take extra pains to guard against it. Also, when you are listening to another student solve a problem, watch his or her approach for errors of the type listed below.

Inaccuracy in Reading

1. Student read the material without concentrating strongly on its meaning. He/she was not careful to understand the problem fully. He/she read sections without realizing that understanding was vague. Did not constantly ask "Do I understand that completely?"

2. Student read the material too rapidly, at the expense of full comprehension.

3. Student missed one or more words (or misread one or more words) because the material was not read carefully enough.

4. Student missed or lost one or more facts or ideas because the material was not read carefully enough.

5. Student did not spend enough time rereading a difficult section to clarify its meaning completely.

Inaccuracy in Thinking

6. Student did not constantly place a high premium on accuracy—did not place accuracy above all other considerations such as speed or ease of obtaining an answer.

7. Student was not sufficiently careful in performing some operation (such as counting letters) or observing some fact (such as which of several figures is the tallest).

8. Student was not consistent in the way he interpreted words or performed operations.

9. Student was uncertain about the correctness of some answer or conclusion, but did not check it.

10. Student was uncertain about whether a formula or procedure used to solve the problem was really appropriate, but did not check it.

11. Student worked too rapidly, which produced errors.

12. Student was inaccurate in visualizing a description or a relationship described in the text.

13. Student drew a conclusion in the middle of the problem without sufficient thought.

Weakness in Problem Analysis; Inactiveness

14. Student did not break a complex problem into parts. Did not begin with a part of the problem that could be handled in order to get a foothold. Did not proceed from one small step to the next small step, being extremely accurate with each one. Did not use the parts of the material he/she could understand to help figure out the more difficult parts. Did not clarify thoughts on the parts understood and then work from there.

15. Student did not draw upon prior knowledge and experience in trying to make sense of ideas which were unclear. He/she did not try to relate the written text to real, concrete events in making the meaning clear and understandable.

16. Student skipped unfamiliar words or phrases, or was satisfied with only a vague understanding of them, rather than trying to obtain a good understanding from the context and the remainder of the material.

17. Student did not translate an unclear word or phrase into own words.

18. Student did not use the dictionary when necessary.

19. Student did not actively construct (mentally or on paper) a representation of ideas described in the text, where such a representation could have helped in understanding the material.

20. Student did not evaluate a solution or interpretation in terms of its reasonableness, i.e., in terms of his prior knowledge about the topic.

Lack of Perseverance

21. Student made little attempt to solve the problem through reasoning because he/she lacked confidence in ability to deal with this type of problem. Took the attitude that reasoning would not work with this problem. Felt confused by the problem, so didn't start systematically by clarifying the portions of the problem that were readily understandable, and then attempting to work from there.

22. Student chose an answer based on only a superficial consideration of the problem—on an impression or feeling about what might be correct. Student made only a superficial attempt to reason the problem, then guessed an answer.

23. Student solved the problem in a mechanical manner, without very much thought.

24. Student reasoned the problem partway through, then gave up and jumped to a conclusion.

Failure to Think Aloud

The items above apply to all academic problem solving. The last item refers specifically to the procedure used in this course.

25. Student did not vocalize thinking in sufficient detail as he or she worked through the problem. At places he/she stopped and thought without vocalizing thoughts. Student performed a numerical computation or drew a conclusion without vocalizing or explaining the steps taken.

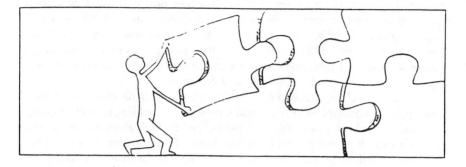

III. PROBLEM-SOLVING METHODS

Introduction

If you are using this book in a class your teacher may ask you to work in pairs as you solve the problems. One partner should read and think aloud, while the other partner listens. On subsequent problems, the partners should change roles, taking turns as problem solver and listener.

You can also use this procedure if you are not in a class, but are working through the book with another person.

Some people find reading and thinking aloud a little awkward at first, but thousands of people have already used this book and have found they adjust to the procedure quickly. Here is the reason that you are asked to read and think aloud.

Thinking Is a Hidden Skill

The ability to analyze complex material and solve problems is a skill—just like any other skill such as the ability to play golf or the ability to drive an automobile. However, there is a peculiar difficulty involved in teaching analytical skill. Generally there are two phases to teaching a skill. First, the skill is demonstrated to the student. Then, the student is guided and corrected while practicing. For example, golf is taught by showing the beginner how to grasp the club, how to place the feet, how to move the arms and body as one swings. The beginner can watch a golf pro—can even watch a slow motion film of the pro in action—and in this way learn the pro's technique. Furthermore, the pro can observe the beginner at practice and point out flaws or demonstrate how to improve.

In contrast to playing golf, analyzing complex material is an activity whcih is generally done inside your head. This makes it somewhat difficult for a teacher to teach and for a learner to learn. In other words, a beginner

21

cannot observe how an expert thinks and solves problems. And the expert has trouble demonstrating technique to a beginning student. There is one way to reduce this difficulty—have people think aloud while they solve problems. If both students and experts vocalize their thoughts as they work through complex ideas and relationships, the steps that they take are open to view and their activities can be observed and communicated.

In this book, the procedure of asking people to think aloud while they solve problems is applied in two ways. Experienced problem solvers (a group of graduate students and professors) were asked to think aloud as they solved the problems that are presented in the book. Their responses were tape-recorded, and then the steps they took in solving a problem were summarized and written out. These summaries are presented under the heading Problem Solution. In other words, the problem solution which follows each problem is a summary of steps taken by an experienced problem solver as he or she worked the problem aloud.

The second application of the procedure consists in asking you, the reader, to think aloud as you work each of the problems. In doing this, you make your thinking visible to other people so that they can observe your attack on a problem. Thus, they can learn the techniques you use; they can help point out any errors you make, and they can compare the steps you take with the steps listed in the problem solution. Furthermore, you will find that by thinking aloud you will be able to look at your own thinking activities more carefully. You will be able to see exactly what strategies you use, and what difficulties you have in solving a problem.

Research has shown that this is an effective way for students to improve their problem-solving skills: work together, think aloud, learn from each other, and read how experienced problem solvers approached the same problems.

Quiz Yourself

1. What are the two phases of teaching a skill such as golf or swimming?

2. What special barrier is met in trying to teach analytical reasoning skill?

3. How has this program attempted to overcome the difficulty encountered in teaching analytical reasoning? How has it handled the two phases of teaching the skill?

Thinking Aloud

In this book, you are asked to do your thinking aloud. Naturally you cannot vocalize all of the mental processing that you do. For example, you cannot explain how you know the meaning of every word you read in a problem. However, when you are unsure about a word or an idea, and you have to stop and think about it, do this thinking aloud. As a rule of thumb, try to think aloud as much as possible while doing the exercises. Spelling out your thoughts—especially at sections of a problem which you find difficult or confusing—is the safest way to insure that you do not skip steps in your reasoning, nor miss facts in drawing conclusions. In other words, you will find that vocalizing your thoughts forces you to be more careful and thorough in analyzing ideas.

Thinking aloud while solving problems requires a certain amount of practice. At first you may find it a little difficult to vocalize your thoughts as you work a problem—to express in words the steps you take in solving the problem. However, research studies show that most students get used to this procedure quickly.

In order to illustrate the procedure of thinking aloud, the response of an experienced problem solver who was asked to think aloud as she worked a problem is reproduced on the following pages.* As you read this protocol, try to follow all of the steps and activities of the problem solver.

Problem Solver's Response

Original Problem

If the circle below is taller than the square and the cross is shorter than the square, put a *K* in the circle. However, if this is not the case, put a *T* in the second tallest figure.

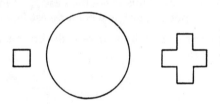

Problem Solver's Response

Note: Read both the comments on the left and the problem solver's report on the right. Quotation marks show when the problem solver read aloud. The absence of quotation marks indicates that the problem solver was thinking aloud.

---

*The problem solver is an outstanding medical student who earned a Master's degree in Comparative Literature before deciding to enter the field of medicine.

The Problem Solver read and thought aloud.

"If the circle below is taller than the square and the cross is shorter than the square, put a *K* in the circle."

Let me start again.

"If the circle below" . . . I'll put my finger on the circle . . . "is taller than the square" . . . Yes, the circle is taller than the square.

"And the cross is shorter than the square" . . . I'll move my finger from the cross to the square and compare them . . . this part is false . . . the cross is not shorter than the square.

"Put a *K* in the circle."

So I shouldn't put a *K* in the circle. Part of the statement is false. I would only write *K* if both the first part and the second part were true.

I should read the whole sentence again and see if my conclusion is correct.

"If the circle is taller than the square" . . . Yes . . . "and the cross is shorter than the square" . . . No . . . "Put a *K* in the circle" . . . I didn't. That's correct.

As the Problem Solver reread the sentence, she moved her finger first from the circle to the square and then from the cross to the square.

I'll continue to the next part of the problem.

"However, if this is not the case" . . . and it isn't the case . . . "put a *T* in the second tallest figure."

The second tallest figure is the cross so I'll put a *T* in the cross.

Another Example

Here is the response that an experienced problem solver (a lawyer) gave to another problem. Note how carefully he checks everything, and even stops for a moment in deciding right from left.

Original Problem

If the word *sentence* contains less than 9 letters and more than 3 vowels, circle the first vowel. Otherwise circle the consonant which is farthest to the right in the word.

Problem Solver's Response

The Problem Solver read the entire problem aloud.	"If the word *sentence* contains less than 9 letters and more than 3 vowels, circle the first vowel. Otherwise circle the consonant which is farthest to the right in the word."
	I'll start from the beginning.
	"If the word *sentence* contains less than 9 letters."
The Problem Solver pointed to the letters with his pen as he counted.	I'll count the letters in *sentence*. *1, 2, 3, 4, 5, 6, 7, 8*. Let me check it. *1, 2, 3, 4, 5, 6, 7, 8*. So it does have less than 9 letters. I'll write the word *yes* above the problem. That way I'll remember it.
The Problem Solver wrote yes over the sentence (see original problem).	
The Problem Solver resumed reading.	"And more than 3 vowels."
The Problem Solver pointed with his pen as he counted.	*1, 2, 3*. Let me check that. *1, 2, 3*. It contains exactly 3 vowels, not more than 3 vowels. I'll write *no* on the problem to remind me.
	"Circle the first vowel."
	So I won't do that.
	"Otherwise circle the consonant which is farthest to the right in the word."
	The consonant farthest to the right? Let me see. Which is my right hand? This is my right hand. OK, so the last letter is the one farthest to the right. But the last letter is *E*. The next letter over is *C*. So it is the consonant farthest to the right. I'll circle the *C*.

Methods of Good Problem Solvers

The Problem Solvers' Responses that you just read illustrate several characteristics of good problem solvers. These characteristics have been studied by researchers and they will be summarized here in five sections.

1. *Positive Attitude*

First of all, good problem solvers have a strong belief that academic reasoning problems can be solved through careful, persistent analysis. Poor problem solvers, by contrast, frequently express the opinion that "either you know the answer to a problem or you don't know it, and if you don't know it you might as well give up or guess." Poor problem solvers haven't learned that a problem may at first appear confusing—that the way to work the problem may not at first be obvious—but that through carefully breaking the problem down, by pinpointing first one piece of information and then another, a difficult problem can be gradually analyzed. Poor problem solvers lack both confidence and experience in dealing with problems through gradual (sometimes lengthy) analysis.

2. *Concern for Accuracy*

Good problem solvers take great care to understand the facts and relationships in a problem fully and accurately. They are almost compulsive in checking whether their understanding of a problem is correct and complete. By contrast, poor problem solvers generally lack such an intense concern about understanding. For example, good problem solvers sometimes reread a problem several times until they are sure they understand it. Poor problem solvers, on the other hand, frequently miss a problem because they do not know exactly what it states. Quite often they could have found out if they had been more careful, if they had reexamined and thought about the problem analytically. But poor problem solvers have not learned how important it is to try to be completely accurate in understanding all of the ideas of a problem. (Recall how the experienced problem solvers in the last two exercises reread sections of the problem to be sure they understood them fully, and rechecked even their simplest calculations.)

3. *Breaking the Problem into Parts*

Good problem solvers have learned that analyzing complex problems and ideas consists of breaking the ideas into smaller steps. They have learned to attack a problem by starting at a point where they can make some sense of it, and then proceeding from there. In contrast, poor problem solvers have not learned the approach of breaking a complex problem into subproblems— dealing first with one step and then another. In the problems which follow, you will see many examples of how complex problems can be worked one step at a time.

4. *Avoiding Guessing*

Poor problem solvers tend to jump to conclusions and guess answers without going through all the steps needed to make sure that the answers are accurate. Sometimes they make intuitive judgments in the middle of a problem without checking to see whether the judgments are correct. At other times they work a problem part of the way, but then give up on reasoning and guess on an answer. Good problem solvers tend to work problems from beginning to end in small, careful steps.

The tendency for poor problem solvers to make more errors—to work too hastily and sometimes skip steps—can be traced to the three characteristics already discussed. First, poor problem solvers do not strongly believe that persistent analysis is an effective way (in fact the only way) to deal with academic reasoning problems. Thus their motivation to persist in working an entire problem precisely and thoroughly—until it is completely solved—is weak.

Second, poor problem solvers tend to be careless in their reasoning. They have not developed the habit of continuously focussing and checking on the accuracy of their conclusions. And third, they have not learned to break a problem into parts and work it step-by-step. As a result of these three characteristics, poor problem solvers have a strong tendency to make hasty responses as they work academic reasoning problems, causing errors in both simple computations and in logic.

5. *Activeness in Problem Solving*

The final characteristic of good problem solvers is the tendency to be more active than poor problem solvers when dealing with academic reasoning problems. Put simply, they do more things as they try to understand and answer difficult questions. For example, if a written description is hard to follow, a good problem solver may try to create a mental picture of the ideas in order to "see" the situation better. If a presentation is lengthy, confusing, or vague, a good problem solver will try to pin it down in terms of familiar experiences and concrete examples. Furthermore, the problem solver will ask questions about the problem, answer the questions, and "talk to him/herself" to clarify thoughts. The problem solver may also count fingers, point to things with a pen, write on the problem, make diagrams, or use other physical aids to thinking. All in all, good problem solvers are active in many ways which improve their accuracy and help them get a clearer understanding of ideas and problems.

Quiz Yourself

The text listed five areas in which good academic problem solvers differ from poor academic problem solvers. These are: 1. motivation and attitude toward problem solving; 2. concern for accuracy; 3. breaking problems into parts; 4. guessing; and 5. activeness in problem solving. Describe and explain three of these areas in detail.

Role of the Listener When Working With a Partner

As noted earlier, if you are using this book in a class your teacher may ask you to work in pairs. One partner should read and think aloud, while the other partner listens. On subsequent problems the partners should change roles, taking turns as problem solver and listener.

The partner who listens plays an important role in the learning process. The listener should not sit back inattentively with his or her mind elsewhere. Instead, the listener should concentrate on two functions: continually checking accuracy and demanding constant vocalization.

1. *Continually Check Accuracy*

Because accuracy is all important, the listener should continually check the accuracy of the problem solver. This includes every computation made, every diagram drawn, every conclusion reached. In other words, the problem solver's accuracy should be checked at every step of the problem, not just at the final answer. For example, if in working the problem shown earlier the problem solver concluded that the word *sentence* has nine letters, the listener should have immediately caught the error and pointed it out.

Catching errors involves several activities. First, the listener must actively work along with the problem solver. The listener should follow every step the problem solver takes, and should be sure to understand each step. If the listener takes a passive attitude—or does not actively think through each step—he or she won't know for sure whether or not the problem solver's steps are totally correct.

Second, the listener should never let the problem solver get ahead of his or her own thinking. This may often mean that the listener will have to ask the problem solver to wait a moment in order to check a conclusion. In this program the emphasis is on accuracy, not on speed. Both the problem solver and the listener should concentrate on accuracy. If the listener needs a moment to verify a conclusion, this will give the problem solver a chance to go over his or her own work and check the thinking. The problem solver should, in the back of the mind, constantly have the thought "is that correct—should I check that?" This will slow down thinking a little so that the listener will be able to keep pace. However, if the problem solver is working too hastily, at the expense of accuracy, the listener should ask him or her to slow down—to follow accurately and analytically. Moreover, even if the problem solver is not working too hastily to be accurate, the listener may still occasionally ask to stop a moment to double-check a point.

Third, the listener should not work the problem separately from the problem solver. When some listeners first learn the procedure used in this program, they turn away from the problem solver and work the problem completely on their own. Occasionally they even finish the problem long before the problem solver. This is incorrect. The listener should listen. This means actively working along with the problem solver, not independently.

Finally, when the listener catches an error, he or she should only point out that an error was made, but should never give the correct answer. By the same token, if the listener sees an answer or a conclusion before the problem solver sees it he or she should *keep quiet*, not furnish it. The listener should wait for the problem solver to work it out. If the problem solver seems completely stuck, the listener may provide a suggestion on the first step to take, but should not actually take the first step or obtain a partial answer. **The problem solver should do all the work.**

In summary, the listener should understand that pointing out errors is not being picky or overly critical. The listener is helping to improve scholastic problem-solving skill—a skill that will be useful in all academic courses. The listener should check every step taken and every conclusion reached by the problem solver. The listener should never let the problem solver go on to a second step without checking the first one. When an error is detected, it should be pointed out without actually being corrected.

2. Demand Constant Vocalization

The second function of the listener is to ensure that the problem solver vocalizes all of the major steps taken in solving a problem. Thinking aloud is a primary part of this program. It is the only way to communicate and to monitor thinking. It should not be neglected. Even the solution of simple problems should be vocalized entirely—so that vocalizing can be done easily when difficult problems are met. If the problem solver skips through one or more steps without thinking aloud, the listener should ask the problem solver to back up and explain the steps.

An Example

The roles of the problem solver and listener are demonstrated in the following dialogue between two graduate students working a problem. As you read through the example, notice how the listener helps the problem solver both to be more accurate and to keep talking. The listener is always following what the problem solver is saying and at the same time looking for ways to make the problem solver think harder about the problem.

Problem Solver

The Problem Solver begins by reading the problem twice.

" 'Bill, Judy and Sally have the occupations of teacher, plumber, and teamster but not necessarily in that order. Bill is shorter than Judy but taller than Sally. The plumber is the tallest and the teamster is the shortest. What is Judy's occupation?' Now you want to see how to solve that? OK. Let's see. I would read it again. 'Bill, Judy and Sally have the occupations of teacher, plumber, and teamster but not necessarily in that order. Bill is shorter than Judy but taller than Sally. The plumber is the tallest and the teamster is the shortest. What is Judy's occupation?' So I would go back to where it says Bill is shorter than Judy but taller than Sally and I would note that in some way. Um, I guess using lines to indicate, you know, some kind of length. No I wouldn't. I would just write their names down in the order that it gives.

Sally < Bill < Judy

So I'd have Bill is less than Judy but taller than Sally—common inequality."

Listener

Here the Listener probably understands the Problem Solver's notation but is looking for a more detailed explanation. It is always a good idea to ask the Listener to explain any new symbol.

"OK. So you're using inequality signs here?"

Problem Solver

"Yeah. Just to show and er, well they indicate height; unequal height. So it could be read the height of Bill is less than the height of Judy and greater than the height of Sally. Then it says the plumber is the tallest of these

teamster_plumber

three so I would write down the word plumber and the teamster is the shortest. And so I . . . where I'd put whatever occupation er, in the middle indicating that the person who is occupied in that manner has the middle height. And then to the left of that I'm going to write teamster."

Listener

The Listener is trying to get the Problem Solver to explain the diagram in more detail.

"Ok. So first you wrote plumber and you put that on the right-hand side?"

Problem Solver

"Right. And then I left a space for some other occupation and then I wrote teamster on the left-hand side, indicating that the teamster is the shortest and the plumber is the tallest."

Listener

Note that while this may seem like a silly question it does get the Problem Solver to reflect more carefully about the problem. In particular, it forces an explicit statement of the implied connection between the two diagrams.

"Why do you put the plumber on the right-hand side? Any reason for that?"

Problem Solver

"No, I could have just as easily put the plumber on the left-hand side except that above it I have the inequality going from right to left meaning that Judy who is the tallest and then Bill who is the next tallest, and then Sally who is the next tallest. So that's probably why I have plumber who is the tallest on the right-hand side under Judy, and teamster who is the shortest on the left-hand side under Sally."

Listener

"Do you think that's why you put it there?"

Problem Solver

"Yeah, I think that's why I put it there. Because I had set the precedent with Sally, less than Bill, less than Judy, going from left to right.

"Uh, so the final question is what is Judy's occupation, and I think that Judy is the plumber." (Pause)

Listener

Whenever the Problem Solver is quiet for more than a few seconds the Listener should ask for verbalization.

"What are you thinking now?"

Problem Solver

"That Judy is the plumber. That Judy is the plumber and I'm going to write um, teacher in between teamster and plumber."

Listener

Even though the Problem Solver seems to have solved the problem, the listener keeps asking questions to make sure the problem is fully understood.

"Why?"

Problem Solver

teamster,
teacher, plumber

"Because I think that uh, the teacher is of medium height. But I'm not sure so I'm going to go and check everything now. Bill, Judy, and Sally have the occupations of teacher, plumber, and teamster but not necessarily in that order, meaning that Bill's not the teacher and Judy's not the plumber and Sally's not the teamster."

Listener

Here the Listener notices that the Problem Solver's words suggest confusion between the terms "not necessarily" and "not." A simple question prompts the Problem Solver to be more careful.

"It means that they're not that?"

Problem Solver

"It says 'but not necessarily in that order,' yeah so Bill does not have to be the teacher. I think when you say 'that order' you mean respectively. You're saying not necessarily respectively. So Bill is not necessarily the teacher."

Listener

"Uh-huh."

Problem Solver

"Judy's not necessarily the plumber and Sally's not necessarily the teamster but it could be that way." (Pause)

Listener

Here again the
Listener prompts
the Problem
Solver to keep
talking.

"So what are you thinking now?"

Problem Solver

"So I was thinking that this inequality that I have written down is correct because it says that Bill is shorter than Judy and taller than Sally. So if Bill is shorter than Judy and taller than Sally, then Judy must also be taller than Sally because Bill is shorter than Judy, and Bill is taller than Sally. So if Judy is taller than Bill then she must be taller than Sally. So I'm fine with that particular statement. The plumber is the tallest and the teamster is the shortest. And since Judy is taller than Bill, and Bill is taller than Sally and then Judy is taller than Sally so Judy is the tallest and the plumber is the tallest and so Judy is the plumber. And the teamster is the shortest and since Sally is let's see—(mumbles to self)—So Judy is shorter than Bill and Judy is shorter than Sally and the teamster is the shortest so I think that Judy is the teamster."

Listener

The Listener tries
to see if the
Problem Solver
notices that this
contradicts the
earlier statement.

"So you just said Judy is the teamster."

Problem Solver

"Right. What did I say before, then, she was the plumber?"

Listener

"Uh-huh."

Problem Solver

"Did I say that?"

Listener

"Yeah."

Problem Solver

"And the teamster is the shortest. No, Sally's the teamster."

Listener

"So what were you just looking at?"

Problem Solver

"Just, you know, momentary dyslexia. Yeah. I'm going to say that Sally's the teamster, and Bill's the teacher and Judy's the plumber."

Listener

The Listener should always check to be sure the Problem Solver is confident before the pair moves on to the next problem.

"Are you sure?"

The previous example involved two skilled students. It is likely that the first time you work a problem the Problem Solver will have a harder time talking. The following example illustrates how the Listener can help get a stubborn Problem Solver to talk more.

Problem

If the second letter in the word *west* comes after the fourth letter in the alphabet, circle the letter A below. If it does not, circle the B.

A   B

*Problem Solver
reads the
problem.*

Problem Solver

" 'If the second letter in the word *west* comes after the fourth letter in alphabet, circle the letter A below. If it does not, circle the B.' "

Listener

"You said 'in alphabet' not 'in *the* alphabet.' "

Problem Solver

"Oh yeah." (Pause)

Listener

"What are you thinking?"

Problem Solver

"Nothing. I am just looking at it." (Pause)

Listener

"What are you looking at?"

Problem Solver

"It's A. I circle the A."

Listener

"Wait a minute. You just said you weren't thinking. Now you say it's A. How did you get that?"

Problem Solver

"Well, the fourth letter is D."

Listener

"Yes."

Problem Solver

"And so I circle the A."

Listener

"How do you get the fourth letter is D?"

Problem Solver

"A, B, C, D. I count."

Listener

"OK. So how come you circle A?"

Problem Solver

"Because that's what it says to do."

Listener

Here the
Listener lies
deliberately.

"I think you are wrong."

Problem Solver

"I am wrong?" (Pause) "You mean it's B. It can't be B because the letter E comes after the letter D."

Listener

"Yeah?"

Problem Solver

"And it says that if the second letter in west, which is e, comes after the fourth letter in the alphabet circle the A. So I did."

Listener

The Listener tests the Problem Solver's confidence by trying another interpretation.

"Yes, but *e* comes before *h*, which is the fourth letter in alphabet."

Problem Solver

"Hmm. You think they want the fourth letter in *alphabet*? (Pause) No they don't, they said *the* alphabet not in alphabet. You pointed that out to me earlier."

Listener

"Oh."

Problem Solver

"So it's A."

Listener

"Wait, tell me all over why you think it is A—go slowly."

Problem Solver

"Well the problem asks you to circle the A if the second letter in *west* which is *e* comes after the fourth letter in the alphabet which is *d*. And *e* does come after *d* so I circle the A."

Listener

"Are you sure?"

Problem Solver

"Yes."

In this example the Listener never gets the Problem Solver to talk in adequate detail, but through a variety of techniques does get the Problem Solver to talk some. With additional practice both students should eventually be able to reach the level of skill demonstrated in the first example.

Summary

As you work problems together, you will see places where the problem solver failed to vocalize his or her thoughts, and you will see errors occurring because of hastiness and failure to recheck. The problem solver may neglect to concentrate fully enough on accuracy, or may forget to approach problems in a systematic, step-by-step manner. Sometimes the errors will be minor, sometimes they will set the problem solution on an entirely wrong track. With experience, you should become sensitive to these types of errors and catch them quickly.

Quiz Yourself

1. What are the two roles of the listener?

2. Describe the activities of the listener in checking for the problem solver's accuracy. According to the text, what are two things the listener should not do?

How Thinking Aloud Pair Problem Solving Works

When you want to learn a new skill there is often a tendency to ask for a complete list of instructions that explains exactly how to perform the task perfectly. But that is not really how learning works. Most learning starts with having a very simple goal in mind and then lots of practice trying to accomplish it. In basketball, you are told the purpose is to get the ball in the basket. After that you get out on the court and learn the details bit by bit through experience. In pottery, someone quickly shows you how to mold clay on a wheel and then you try your hand at it. Over the years you may pick up hundreds of hours in instruction but most of this comes in the form of short hints delivered during the course of your practice. Most of your learning comes not from what other people tell you, but from your own ability to notice what works well and what does not.

Thinking Aloud Pair Problem Solving is a very simple process that will become increasingly complex and sophisticated as your experience with it develops. Initially, all you need to know is that the problem solver must explain every step in her reasoning and that the listener has to understand every step that the problem solver takes. From these two simple goals everything else follows. Teachers and this book can give hints here and there but the vast majority of learning will come from the dynamic of the process itself. Every time you are a listener you are learning about problem solving by paying careful attention to what the problem solver does and does not do. Every time you are the problem solver you are indirectly observing the listener who is listening to you. The process has built into it all the feedback you need.

If in the middle of a basketball game you were to forget that the purpose is to score baskets, you would quickly lose the feedback you need to improve your game. Likewise, in TAPPS if you forget that the purpose is to better understand thinking, then you will cut off your learning feedback and the opportunity to improve your skills. Solving the problems quickly and correctly is not the major purpose of TAPPS. It is only through being able to better understand your own reasoning as well as that of others, that you will become a better thinker and a better problem solver. In the long run being a better problem solver will increase your speed and accuracy but making these short-term goals will only serve to limit your learning.

Thus, there is only one thing you need to remember in Thinking Aloud Pair Problem Solving. The goal is to better understand thinking, your own and other people's. Keep that goal in mind and everything else will follow.

Problem Solutions

Many of the problems in this book are followed by a section labeled Problem Solution. The problem solution breaks the problem into a series of steps and shows how the problem can be solved in a step-by-step manner. The steps were obtained by asking good problem solvers to think aloud as they worked the problems and then summarizing their steps so they would be easy to read.

After you and your partner agree on the answer to a problem, turn to the problem solution to check that the answer is correct. The steps which are listed may not be identical to the way in which you solved the problem, but the final answer should be the same. If you had any difficulty with the problem, review all the steps in the solution to see whether they differ from the approach you used.

Your instructor may give quizzes in problem solving, asking you to solve problems similar to the ones in the book. Therefore, it will be worth your while to look over the problem solutions carefully to insure you can solve all the problems effectively.

Devising Problems

For homework and additional classwork, your instructor will ask you to devise problems similar to certain of the ones in this chapter. Devising problems based on other problems allows you to see them from the inside out. You come to understand how the various parts of the problems operate and how they relate to each other. Don't be surprised to find that devising good problems can require much more thinking than solving them. Just take your time changing the various problem elements until you are totally satisfied.

Devise each problem on your own. Then have another student solve it, reading and thinking aloud, and also writing out all the steps in the solution.

Check to be sure no steps are skipped. The solution should be as complete as solutions you read in earlier sections of this book. Writing out complete solutions is a powerful exercise for strengthening problem-solving skills as well as writing skills.

Place just one problem per page so that the solution can be written below it. Make the problems difficult enough to be challenging. But be certain they are logically sound and solvable before asking other students to work them.

Awareness and Communication of Thinking: Pre-test

Two objectives of this workbook are increasing your awareness of the mental activities you use in solving problems and improving your ability to explain these mental activities. Becoming more aware of your mental activities will help you interpret and organize information; keep track of where you are while solving a problem; identify obstacles when you are stuck; and increase your accuracy. Use the diagram below to rate yourself on awareness of mental activities. At the end of the next chapter you will rate yourself again so you can evaluate your progress.

*Awareness**

How aware are you of the process you use to solve problems? Use an "x" to indicate your assessment.

```
0     1     2     3     4     5     6     7     8     9     10
|     |     |     |     |     |     |     |     |     |     |
```

Unaware.   Aware of some   Very aware.
I just do it.   I can describe the
                                                   details of how I do it

*From *The McMaster Problem Solving Program: Unit I, Developing Awareness* by Donald R. Woods. Department of Chemical Engineering, McMaster University, Hamilton, Ontario, Canada, 1985, by permission of the author.

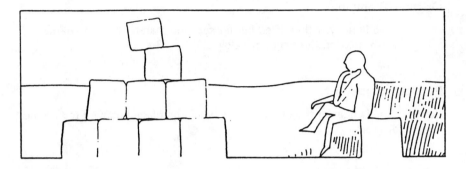

IV. VERBAL REASONING PROBLEMS

Introduction

In this chapter each problem is followed by a problem solution. Scan the solution to see if your answer is correct. If it is not correct, read the entire problem solution aloud. As you read the solution, notice how the problem is analyzed into steps. Also notice any diagrams or other problem-solving aids and techniques that are employed. Make use of these techniques whenever they are appropriate in solving later problems.

Problem 1

José is heavier than Fred but lighter than Marty. Write the names of the 3 men on the diagram below.

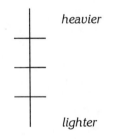

heavier

lighter

Original Problem

José is heavier than Fred but lighter than Marty. Write the names of the 3 men on the diagram below.

Problem Solution

Step 1. José is heavier than Fred . . . He would be placed above Fred on the diagram.

José ─┼─

Fred ─┼─

Step 2. . . . but lighter than Marty.

This says José is lighter than Marty. So Marty is placed above José on the diagram.

Marty ─┼─

José ─┼─

Fred ─┼─

Problem 2

Jack is slower than Phil but faster than Val. Val is slower than Jack but faster than Pete. Write the names of the 4 men in order on the diagram below.

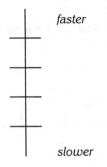

faster

slower

Original Problem

Jack is slower than Phil but faster than Val. Val is slower than Jack but faster than Pete. Write the names of the 4 men in order on the diagram below.

Problem Solution

Step 1. Jack is slower than Phil . . . He would be placed below Phil.

Phil ┼
│
Jack ┼

Step 2. . . . but faster than Val.

This says Jack is faster than Val. So Val is added below Jack.

Phil ┼
Jack ┼
Val ┼

Step 3. Val is slower than Jack . . .
This is already represented in the diagram.

Step 4. . . . but faster than Pete.

Val is faster than Pete, so Pete is added to the diagram below Val.

Phil ┼
Jack ┼
Val ┼
Pete ┼

Problem 3

If Dumani and Fred are both richer than Tom, and Hal is poorer than Dumani but richer than Fred, which man is the poorest and which one is the next poorest? Write the names of all 4 men in order on the diagram.

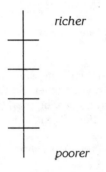

richer

poorer

Original Problem

> If Dumani and Fred are both richer than Tom, and Hal is poorer than Dumani but richer than Fred, which man is the poorest and which one is the next poorest? Write the names of all 4 men in order on the diagram.

Problem Solution

Step 1. If Dumani and Fred are both richer than Tom . . .

Dumani ? Fred

Tom

The problem does not indicate whether Dumani and Fred are actually equal to each other. So they are represented on the diagram with a question mark between them, and with both of them above Tom.

Step 2. . . . while Hal is poorer than Dumani but richer than Fred . . .

Dumani

Hal

Fred

Tom

This means that Dumani and Fred are not equal; Hal is between them, with Dumani the richest.

Tom is the poorest and Fred is next poorest.

Problem 4

Paul and Tom are the same age. Paul is older than Cynthia. Cynthia is younger than Hal. Is Paul older or younger than Hal—or can this not be determined from the information?

Original Problem

Paul and Tom are the same age. Paul is older than Cynthia. Cynthia is younger than Hal. Is Paul older or younger than Hal—or can this not be determined from the information?

Problem Solution

Step 1. Paul and Tom are the same age. Paul is   Paul = Tom
older than Cynthia.   Cynthia

This can be represented in a diagram.

Step 2. Cynthia is younger than Hal.

This says Hal is older than Cynthia. But it $\text{Paul} = \text{Tom}\genfrac{}{}{0pt}{}{?}{?} \Big\} \text{Hal}$
doesn't indicate whether Hal is older or
younger than Paul and Tom. This is indicated   Cynthia
with a bracket on the diagram.

Step 3. Is Paul older or younger than Hal—or
can this not be determined from the
information?

It cannot be determined.

Problem 5

Cathy knows French and Farci, Nomsa knows Xosha and Chinese, Cindy knows Spanish and French, and Parvati knows Farci and Xosha. If French is easier than Farci, Chinese is harder than Xosha, Farci is easier than Xosha, and Spanish is easier than French, which girl knows the most difficult languages?

Original Problem

Cathy knows French and Farci, Nomsa knows Xosha and Chinese,
Cindy knows Spanish and French, and Parvati knows Farci and Xosha.
If French is easier than Farci, Chinese is harder than Xosha, Farci is
easier than Xosha, and Spanish is easier than French, which girl
knows the most difficult languages?

Problem Solution

Step 1. Strategy for beginning the problem: The question asks
which girl knows the most difficult languages.
Therefore the first step is to order the languages by
difficulty. This information is contained in the second
sentence of the problem, so the solution starts with
the second sentence.

Step 2. If French is easier than Farci . . .

This can be shown in a diagram. The easier language
has been arbitrarily put below the harder language.

Farci
French

Step 3. . . . Chinese is harder than Xosha.

This can be shown in a separate diagram.

Chinese
Xosha

Step 4. Farci is easier than Xosha . . .

This information shows how the two diagrams can be
combined. Farci is placed below Xosha since it is
easier.

Chinese
Xosha
Farci
French

Step 5. . . . Spanish is easier than French.

This can be added to the diagram.

Chinese
Xosha
Farci
French
Spanish

Step 6. The diagram shows that Chinese and Xosha are the
two most difficult languages. In order to answer the
question it is necessary to find the girl who speaks
these two languages. Scanning the first sentence
shows that Nomsa speaks them.

Nomsa speaks Chinese and Xosha, the most difficult
languages.

Problem 6

Hom, Sam, and Ricardo differ in height. Their last names are Smith, Su, and Calvin, but not necessarily in that order. Hom is taller than Ricardo but shorter than Sam. Smith is the tallest of the 3 and Calvin is the shortest. What are Hom's and Ricardo's last names?

Original Problem

Hom, Sam, and Ricardo differ in height. Their last names are Smith, Su, and Calvin, but not necessarily in that order. Hom is taller than Ricardo but shorter than Sam. Smith is the tallest of the 3 and Calvin is the shortest. What are Hom's and Ricardo's last names?

Problem Solution

Step 1. Strategy for beginning the problem: Information is given about the heights of the men in terms of their first names and in terms of their last names. By diagramming both sets of relationships, the first names can be matched up with the last names.

Step 2. Hom is taller than Ricardo . . .

This is represented in the diagram on the right.

Hom ┼
Ricardo ┼

Step 3. . . . but shorter than Sam.

This says Hom is shorter than Sam, so Sam is added above diagram.

Sam ┼
Hom ┼
Ricardo ┼

Step 4. Smith is the tallest of the 3 and Calvin is the shortest.

This information can be represented in a new diagram referring to the men's last names. A blank space is left for the third man's name.

Smith ┼

Calvin ┼

Step 5. Scanning the problem shows that the third man's last name is Su, so this can be added to the diagram.

Smith ┼
Su ┼
Calvin ┼

Step 6. Comparing the 2 diagrams shows that:

Hom's last name is Su.
Ricardo's last name is Calvin.

Problem 7

Three fathers—Pete, John, and Nick—have between them a total of 15 children of which 9 are boys. Pete has 3 girls and John has the same number of boys. John has 1 more child than Pete, who has 4 children. Nick has 4 more boys than girls and the same number of girls as Pete has boys. How many boys each do Nick and Pete have?

Hint: It may be helpful to arrange the information into a table of the type shown below.

	Boys	Girls	Total
Pete John Nick Total			

Original Problem

Three fathers—Pete, John, and Nick—have between them a total of 15 children of which 9 are boys. Pete has 3 girls and John has the same number of boys. John has 1 more child than Pete who has 4 children. Nick has 4 more boys than girls and the same number of girls as Pete has boys. How many boys each do Nick and Pete have?

Problem Solution

Step 1. Three fathers—Pete, John, and Nick—have between them a total of 15 children of which 9 are boys.

	Boys	Girls	Total
Pete			
John			
Nick			
Total	9		15

Step 2. The table shows that there are 9 boys and a total of 15 children. So there must be 6 girls.

	Boys	Girls	Total
Pete			
John			
Nick			
Total	9	6	15

Step 3. Pete has 3 girls and John has the same number of boys.

	Boys	Girls	Total
Pete		3	
John	3		
Nick			
Total	9	6	15

Step 4. John has 1 more child than Pete who has 4 children. This means John has 5 children.

	Boys	Girls	Total
Pete		3	4
John	3		5
Nick			
Total	9	6	15

Step 5. The table shows that Pete has 4 children, of which 3 are girls, so he must have 1 boy. Also, John must have 2 girls; and Nick must have 6 children since Pete and John together have 9 children.

	Boys	Girls	Total
Pete	1	3	4
John	3	2	5
Nick			6
Total	9	6	15

Step 6. Looking at the last table shows that Pete and John together have 4 boys, so Nick must have 5 boys. Also, Nick must have 1 girl.

	Boys	Girls	Total
Pete	1	3	4
John	3	2	5
Nick	5	1	6
Total	9	6	15

Step 7. The table is filled in, but there is one sentence of information remaining. It can be read and checked against the table to make sure that the table is correct.

Nick has 4 more boys and the same number of girls as Pete has boys.

The table shows that Nick has 5 boys and 1 girl—so he does have 4 more boys than girls. The table is correct on this point. Also, Nick has 1 girl and Pete has 1 boy, so this is correct.

Step 8. How many boys each do Nick and Pete have?

The table shows: Nick has 5 boys.
                 Pete has 1 boy.

Problem 8

Paula, Joanne, and Mary own a total of 16 dogs, among which are 3 poodles, twice that many cocker spaniels, and the remainder German shepherds and collies. Joanne despises poodles and collies, but owns 4 cocker spaniels and 2 German shepherds, giving her a total of 6 dogs. Paula owns 1 poodle and only 2 other dogs, both German shepherds. Mary owns 3 collies and several other dogs. What other dogs (and how many of each) does Mary own?

Note: In constructing a table for this problem, remember to enter zeros as well as positive numbers whenever appropriate. Some students forget to enter zeros and therefore think this problem cannot be solved. Also, enter totals as soon as you can. For example, enter the total of 16 dogs now.

Original Problem

Paula, Joanne, and Mary own a total of 16 dogs, among which are poodles, twice that many cocker spaniels, and the remainder German shepherds and collies. Joanne despises poodles and collies, but owns 4 cocker spaniels and 2 German shepherds, giving her a total of 6 dogs. Paula owns 1 poodle and only 2 other dogs, both German shepherds. Mary owns 3 collies and several other dogs. What other dogs (and how many of each) does Mary own?

Problem Solution

Step 1. Paula, Joanne, and Mary own a total of 16 dogs, among which are 3 poodles, twice that many cocker spaniels and the remainder German shepherds and collies.

	Poodle	Spaniel	Shepherd	Collie	Total
Paula					
Joanne					
Mary					
Total	3	6			16

Step 2. Joanne despises poodles and collies, but owns 4 cocker spaniels and 2 German shepherds.

	Poodle	Spaniel	Shepherd	Collie	Total
Paula					
Joanne	0	4	2	0	6
Mary					
Total	3	6			16

Step 3. Paula owns 1 poodle and only 2 other dogs, both German shepherds.

	Poodle	Spaniel	Shepherd	Collie	Total
Paula	1	0	2	0	3
Joanne	0	4	2	0	6
Mary					
Total	3	6			16

Step 4. Since Paula and Joanne own 9 dogs between them, and there are a total of 16 dogs, Mary must own 7 dogs. Also, since Paula and Joanne have only 1 poodle between them, Mary must own 2 poodles. Again, Mary must own 2 spaniels since Paula and Joanne have 4 between them. This is shown in the next table.

	Poodle	Spaniel	Shepherd	Collie	Total
Paula	1	0	2	0	3
Joanne	0	4	2	0	6
Mary	2	2			7
Total	3	6			16

Step 5. Mary owns 3 collies and several other dogs.

	Poodle	Spaniel	Shepherd	Collie	Total
Paula	1	0	2	0	3
Joanne	0	4	2	0	6
Mary	2	2		3	7
Total	3	6			16

Step 6. The table shows there are a total of 3 collies. Thus there must be 4 shepherds. This means that Mary owns no shepherds.

	Poodle	Spaniel	Shepherd	Collie	Total
Paula	1	0	2	0	3
Joanne	0	4	2	0	6
Mary	2	2	0	3	7
Total	3	6	4	3	16

Step 7. What other dogs (and how many of each) does Mary own?

The table shows Mary owns 2 poodles and 2 cocker spaniels in addition to her collies.

Problem 9

Sales agents who work for the Acme Wig Company are assigned to a different city each year. Henry began working for Acme in New York in 1995, and in the succeeding 4 years worked in Minneapolis, New Haven, Youngstown, and Charleston, in that order. Martha worked for Acme in New Haven in 1993, and in succeeding years worked in New York, Charleston, Minneapolis, and Youngstown. Fred worked for Acme in Charleston in 1997; the previous 2 years he had worked first in New Haven and then in Minneapolis. John worked in Charleston in 1998. Before that he was in New Haven, before that Youngstown, and before that New York. Which Acme sales agents were in New Haven in 1997. Which ones were in Minneapolis in 1996?

Original Problem

Sales agents who work for the Acme Wig Company are assigned to a different city each year. Henry began working for Acme in New York in 1995, and in the succeeding 4 years worked in Minneapolis, New Haven, Youngstown and Charleston, in that order. Martha worked for Acme in New Haven in 1993, and in succeeding years worked in New York, Charleston, Minneapolis and Youngstown. Fred worked for Acme in Charleston in 1997; the previous 2 years he had worked first in New Haven and then in Minneapolis. John worked in Charleston in 1998. Before that he was in New Haven, before that Youngstown, and before that New York. Which Acme sales agents were in New Haven in 1997? Which ones were in Minneapolis in 1996?

Problem Solution

Two ways of organizing the information are shown in tables below:

	Henry	Martha	Fred	John
1993		New Haven		
1994		New York		
1995	New York	Charleston	New Haven	New York
1996	Minneapolis	Minneapolis	Minneapolis	Youngstown
1997	New Haven	Youngstown	Charleston	New Haven
1998	Youngstown			Charleston
1999	Charleston			

	Henry	Martha	Fred	John
New York	1995	1994		1995
Minneapolis	1996	1996	1996	
New Haven	1997	1993	1995	1997
Youngstown	1998	1997		1996
Charleston	1999	1995	1997	1998

Both tables show that Henry and John were in New Haven in 1997, and that Henry, Martha, and Fred were in Minneapolis in 1996.

Problem 10

On a certain day I ate lunch at Tommy's, took out 2 books from the library (*The Sea Wolf* and *Martin Eden*, both by Jack London), visited the museum, and had a cavity filled. Tommy's is closed on Wednesday, the library is closed on weekends, the museum is only open Monday, Wednesday, and Friday, and my dentist has office hours Tuesday, Friday, and Saturday. On which day of the week did I do all these things?

Original Problem

On a certain day I ate lunch at Tommy's, took out 2 books from the library (*The Sea Wolf* and *Martin Eden*, both by Jack London), visited the museum, and had a cavity filled. Tommy's is closed on Wednesday, the library is closed on weekends, the museum is only open Monday, Wednesday, and Friday, and my dentist has office hours Tuesday, Friday, and Saturday. On which day of the week did I do all these things?

Problem Solution

Step 1. Suggestion for beginning the problem: The restrictions on when these activities occurred are stated in the second sentence.

Step 2. Tommy's is closed on Wednesday . . .

S   M   T   W̸   TH   F   SAT

Step 3. . . . the library is closed on weekends . . .

S̸   M   T   W̸   TH   F   S̸A̸T̸

Step 4. . . . the museum is only open Monday, Wednesday, and Friday . . . This means it is closed the other days.

S̸   M   T̸   W̸   T̸H̸   F   S̸A̸T̸

Step 5. . . . and my dentist has office hours Tuesday, Friday, and Saturday. This eliminates Monday.

S̸   M̸   T̸   W̸   T̸H̸   F   S̸A̸T̸

Step 6. On which day of the week did I do all these things?

Friday.

Problem 11

Boris, Irwin, and Steven are engaged in the occupations of librarian, teacher, and electrician, although not necessarily in that order. The librarian is Steven's cousin. Irwin lives next door to the electrician. Boris, who knows more facts than the teacher, must drive 45 minutes to visit Irwin's house.

What is each man's occupation?

It is helpful to use a table like the one shown below. Here is step 1 in the solution.

Step 1. The problem says the librarian is Steven's cousin. That means Steven is not the librarian. This is shown by writing "NO" in the table.

	librarian	teacher	electrician
Boris			
Irwin			
Steven	NO		

Complete the table and determine each man's occupation.

Original Problem

Boris, Irwin, and Steven are engaged in the occupations of librarian, teacher and electrician, although not necessarily in that order. The librarian is Steven's cousin. Irwin lives next door to the electrician. Boris, who knows more facts than the teacher, must drive 45 minutes to visit Irwin's house.

Problem Solution

Step 1. The problem says the librarian is Steven's cousin. That means Steven is not the librarian. This is shown by writing "NO" in the table.

	librarian	teacher	electrician
Boris			
Irwin			
Steven	NO		

Step 2. Irwin lives next door to the electrician. This means Irwin is not the electrician.

	librarian	teacher	electrician
Boris			
Irwin			NO
Steven	NO		

Step 3. "Boris, who knows more facts than the teacher, . . ." This means Boris is not the teacher.

	librarian	teacher	electrician
Boris		NO	
Irwin			NO
Steven	NO		

Step 4. "... must drive 45 minutes to visit Irwin's house."

An earlier sentence said Irwin lives next door to the electrician. Since Boris must drive 45 minutes to visit Irwin, he is not the electrician.

	librarian	teacher	electrician
Boris		NO	NO
Irwin			NO
Steven	NO		

Step 5. From the table we see that Boris must be the librarian.

	librarian	teacher	electrician
Boris	YES	NO	NO
Irwin			NO
Steven	NO		

Step 6. The table also shows that Steven must be the electrician.

	librarian	teacher	electrician
Boris	YES	NO	NO
Irwin			NO
Steven	NO		YES

Step 7. Irwin must be the teacher.

Problem 12

Three men—Fred, Ed, and Ted—are married to Joan, Sally, and Vickie, but not necessarily in that order. Joan, who is Ed's sister, lives in Detroit. Fred dislikes animals. Ed weighs more than the man who is married to Vickie. The man married to Sally breeds Siamese cats as a hobby. Fred commutes over 200 hours a year from his home in Ann Arbor to his job in Detroit. Match up the men with the women they married.

Original Problem

Three men—Fred, Ed, and Ted—are married to Joan, Sally and Vickie, but not necessarily in that order. Joan, who is Ed's sister, lives in Detroit. Fred dislikes animals. Ed weighs more than the man who is married to Vickie. The man married to Sally breeds Siamese cats as a hobby. Fred commutes over 200 hours a year from his home in Ann Arbor to his job in Detroit. Match up the men with the women they married.

Problem Solution

Step 1. The problem says Joan is Ed's sister. Therefore Joan and Ed are not married.

	Joan	Sally	Vickie
Fred			
Ed	NO		
Ted			

Step 2. The problem says Joan lives in Detroit, and Fred dislikes animals. There is no way to use that information yet.

The next statement says Ed weighs more than the man who is married to Vickie. That means Ed is not married to Vickie.

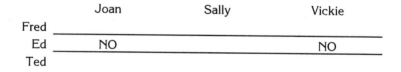

	Joan	Sally	Vickie
Fred			
Ed	NO		NO
Ted			

Step 3. The table shows that Ed must be married to Sally.

	Joan	Sally	Vickie
Fred			
Ed	NO	YES	NO
Ted			

Step 4. Since Ed is married to Sally, we know that neither Fred nor Ted is married to Sally.

	Joan	Sally	Vickie
Fred		NO	
Ed	NO	YES	NO
Ted		NO	

Step 5. The problem says that the man married to Sally breeds Siamese cats as a hobby. Earlier the problem said that Fred dislikes animals. That means that Fred is not married to Sally. This is already shown in the table.

Step 6. The problem says that Fred commutes from his home in Ann Arbor to his job in Detroit. Earlier it said Joan lives in Detroit. Therefore we can conclude that Fred is not married to Joan.

	Joan	Sally	Vickie
Fred	NO	NO	
Ed	NO	YES	NO
Ted		NO	

Step 7. Fred must be married to Vickie.

Joan must be married to Ted.

Problem 13

You are facing east, you turn to face the opposite direction, and then you turn 90% left. Which direction is now on your left side?

Original Problem

You are facing east, you turn to face the opposite direction, and then you turn 90% left. Which direction is now on your left side?

Problem Solution

Step 1. A useful aid in solving a problem like this in your head (without making a diagram) is to picture yourself standing on some map with which you are familiar. The following solution uses a map of the United States.

Step 2. You are facing east . . .

On a map of the United States you would be facing the Atlantic Ocean, with Canada on your left and the southern states such as Florida and Texas on your right.

Step 3. . . . you turn to face the opposite direction . . .

You might turn left, past Canada, and face California.

Step 4. . . . and then you turn left 90%.

You turn south facing Texas.

Step 5. Which direction is now on your left side?

If you are facing south, the east coast is on your left.

East is on your left.

Problem 14

A train left city *A* at 9:35 and arrived at city *B* 5 hours and 40 minutes later. What time did it arrive at city *B*?

Original Problem

A train left city *A* at 9:35 and arrived at city *B* 5 hours and 40 minutes later. What time did it arrive at city *B*?

Problem Solution

Step 1. 9:35 plus 3 hours is 12:35.

Step 2. 12:35 plus 2 more hours is 2:35.

Step 3. 2:35 plus 40 minutes is 2:75.

Step 4. 2:75 is 3:15. (Since there are 60 minutes in 1 hour.) The train arrived at 3:15.

Problem 15

Belvedere Street is parallel to St. Anthony Street. Davidson Street is perpendicular to River Street. River Street is parallel to St. Anthony Street. Is Davidson Street parallel or perpendicular to Belvedere?

Original Problem

Belvedere Street is parallel to St. Anthony Street. Davidson Street is perpendicular to River Street. River Street is parallel to St. Anthony Street. Is Davidson Street parallel or perpendicular to Belvedere?

Problem Solution

Step 1. Belvedere Street is parallel to St. Anthony Street.

Belvedere

St. Anthony

Step 2. Davidson Street is perpendicular to River Street.

This sentence presents information on two new streets. It can be skipped over temporarily.

Step 3. River Street is parallel to St. Anthony Street.

This can be added to the above diagram.

Belvedere

St. Anthony

River

Step 4. Now, going back to the second sentence: Davidson Street is perpendicular to River Street.

This can now be added to the diagram.

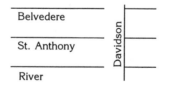

Step 5. Is Davidson Street parallel or perpendicular to Belvedere?

The diagram shows that Davidson is perpendicular.

Problem 16

In the town of Pottsville, streets with names that begin with a vowel and end with a consonant run north-south. Those which begin with a consonant and end with a vowel run east-west. Others may run either way. If Carter Street is perpendicular to Agnes Street, is it parallel or perpendicular to Sheridan Street, which runs north-south?

Original Problem

In the town of Pottsville, streets with names that begin with a vowel and end with a consonant run north-south. Those which begin with a consonant and end with a vowel run east-west. Others may run either way. If Carter Street is perpendicular to Agnes Street, is it parallel or perpendicular to Sheridan Street, which runs north-south?

Problem Solution

Step 1. The question concerns the relationship between Carter and Sheridan.

Step 2. Sheridan runs north-south.

Step 3. Carter begins with a consonant and ends with a consonant so it can run either way.

Step 4. Agnes begins with a vowel and ends with a consonant so it runs north-south.

Step 5. The problem says Carter is perpendicular to Agnes.

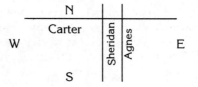

Step 6. The diagram shows that Carter Street is perpendicular to Sheridan.

Problem 17

How many letters are in either the rectangle or the square, but not in both?

Note: The problem says nothing about the circle. Therefore treat the circle as if were not there. A simple example illustrates this idea. If an instructor asked all blue-eyed students to stand up, it would mean both *tall* and *short* blue-eyed students. Since height is not mentioned, it should be ignored in this situation.

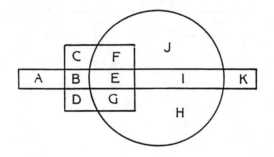

Original Problem

How many letters are in either the rectangle or the square, but not in both?

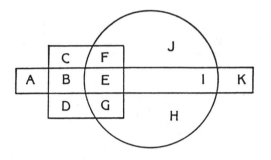

Problem Solution

A is in just the rectangle.
C is in just the square.
D is in just the square.
G is in just the square (ignoring the circle).
F is in just the square (ignoring the circle).
I is in just the rectangle (ignoring the circle).
K is in just the rectangle.

There are 7 letters in either the rectangle or the square, but not in both.

Problem 18

In working this problem, consider the diagram to be made up of 3 major geometrical figures. *1.* a triangle; *2.* a circle; and *3.* a rectangle. How many letters are in exactly 2 (but not 3) of these figures?

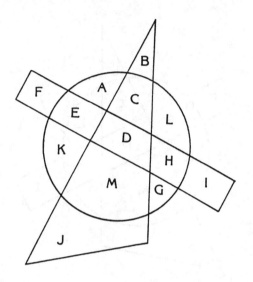

Original Problem

In working this problem, consider the diagram to be made up of 3 major geometrical figures: *1.* a triangle; *2.* a circle; and *3.* a rectangle. How many letters are in exactly 2 (but not 3) of these figures?

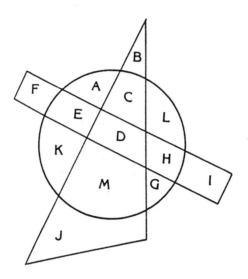

Problem Solution

E is in the circle and the rectangle.
C is in the triangle and the circle.
H is in the circle and the rectangle.
M is in the circle and the triangle.

There are 4 letters in exactly 2 figures.

Problem 19

In working this problem, consider the diagram to be made up of 5 major geometrical figures: *1.* 1 triangle; *2.* 2 circles; and *3.* 2 rectangles. List the letters which are in the same number of major geometrical figures as the letter G. List them here _____.

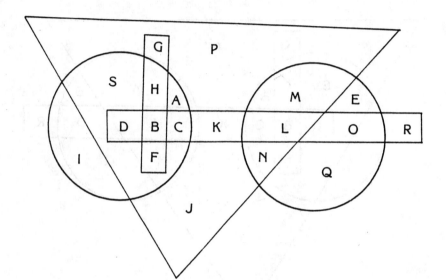

Original Problem

In working this problem, consider the diagram to be made up of 5 major geometrical figures: *1.* 1 triangle; *2.* 2 circles; and *3.* 2 rectangles. List the letters which are in the same number of major geometrical figures as the letter *G*. List them here _____.

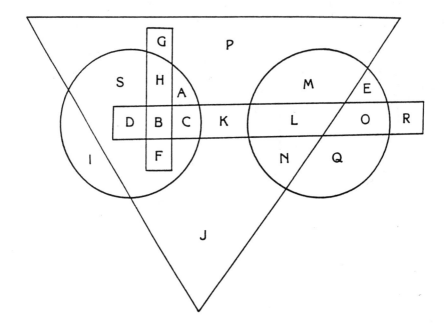

Problem Solution

Step 1. The letter *G* is in the triangle and also in 1 of the rectangles. So it is in 2 major geometrical figures.

Step 2. S is in the triangle and 1 of the circles.

A is in the triangle and 1 of the circles.

K is in the triangle and 1 of the rectangles.

N is in the triangle and 1 of the circles.

M is in the triangle and 1 of the circles.

O is in 1 of the rectangles and 1 of the circles.

The next group of problems employ Venn diagrams. Here is the way Venn diagrams can be used to represent certain statements.

Example *a*. All A are B. (For instance, all dogs are animals.)

Example *b*. No C are D. (For instance, no people are cars.)

Example *c*. Some E are F. (For instance, some women are Democrats.)

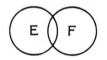

Problem 20

Problem: Make a Venn diagram with 3 circles showing the following relationships.

Some x are y. No x are z. No y are z.

Original Problem

Make a Venn diagram with 3 circles showing the following relationships.

Some x are y. No x are z. No y are z.

Problem Solution

Problem 21

Make a Venn diagram with 3 circles showing the following relationships.

Some x are y. Some x are z. No y are z.

Original Problem

Make a Venn diagram with 3 circles showing the following relation-ships.

Some x are y. Some x are z. No y are z.

Problem Solution

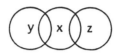

Problem 22

Make a Venn diagram showing the relationships between cats, animals, and cars, using one circle to represent cats, another to represent animals, and a third to represent cars.

Original Problem

> Make a Venn diagram showing the relationships between cats, animals, and cars, using one circle to represent cats, another to represent animals, and a third to represent cars.

Problem Solution

Problem 23

Make a Venn diagram showing the relationships between cats, dogs, and animals.

Original Problem

Make a Venn diagram showing the relationships between cats, dogs, and animals.

Problem Solution

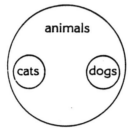

Problem 24

If some of Totteville's residents have brown eyes and some of Totteville's residents are women, is the statement "Some of Totteville's residents are brown-eyed women" true, false, or unsubstantiated?

Original Problem

If some of Totteville's residents have brown eyes and some of Totteville's residents are women, is the statement "Some of Totteville's residents are brown-eyed women" true, false, or unsubstantiated?

Problem Solution

From the statement we can't tell whether none of the brown-eyed residents are women (as shown in diagram 1) or whether some of the brown-eyed residents are women (as shown in diagram 2).

Therefore the statement is not definitely false (diagram 1) or definitely true (diagram 2). It is just unsubstantiated.

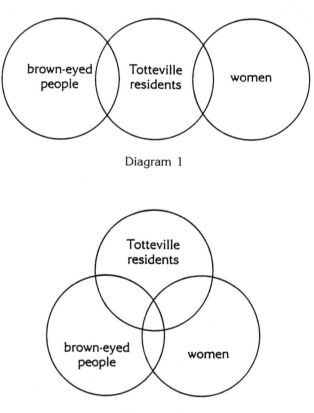

Diagram 1

Diagram 2

Problem 25

For this problem, assume the first two statements are correct and make a diagram to represent the relationships.* Then answer the questions.

All bears are butterflies. All bees are bears.

a. Can you be certain that all bees are butterflies?

b. Can you be certain that all butterflies are bees?

*This question presents an example of assuming something to be true in order to see what relationships and possibilities would result. It is a form of "hypothetical reasoning." Here we are redefining the common words "bees," "bears," and "butterflies" to represent new classes of things having the relationships specified in the first two sentences of the problem. This type of question exercises the mind in that one has to put aside standard knowledge and mentally construct new definitions and relationships in order to solve the problem.

Original Problem

For this problem, assume the first two statements are correct and make a diagram to represent the relationships. Then answer the questions.

All bears are butterflies. All bees are bears.

a. Can you be certain that all bees are butterflies?

b. Can you be certain that all butterflies are bees?

Problem Solution

Here is the diagram showing that all bees are bears and all bears are butterflies.

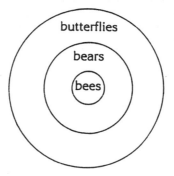

Answer for question a.   The diagram shows that all bees are butterflies. Anything in the circle for bees is automatically in the circle for butterflies.

Answer for question b.   The diagram shows that there can be butterflies which are not bees. For example, the dot in the diagram below is a butterfly that is not a bee.

This is a butterfly that is not a bee.

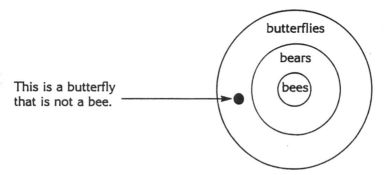

Problem 26

The fire department wants to send booklets on fire hazards to all teachers and homeowners in town. How many booklets does it need, using these statistics? Use a Venn diagram in solving this problem.

Homeowners. 50,000
Teachers. 4,000
Teachers who own their homes 3,000

Original Problem

The fire department wants to send booklets on fire hazards to all teachers and homeowners in town. How many booklets does it need, using these statistics?

Homeowners 50,000
Teachers 4,000
Teachers who own their homes. 3,000

Problem Solution

Step 1. The left circle is the homeowners. The right circle is the teachers.

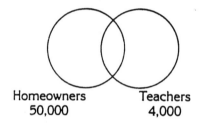

Step 2. Three thousand people are both homeowners and teachers.

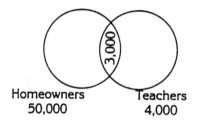

Step 3. The remaining portions of the circles can be filled in.

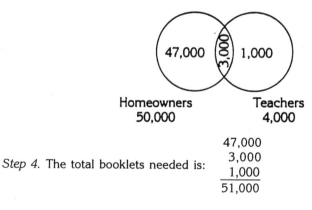

Step 4. The total booklets needed is:

        47,000
         3,000
         1,000
        ——————
        51,000

Problem 27

An insurance company wants to contact all physicians and all licensed drivers in town. Using these statistics, how many people must be contacted? Draw a Venn diagram with your solution.

Licensed drivers 8,000
Physicians. 750
Physicians with drivers licenses 750

Original Problem

An insurance company wants to contact all physicians and all licensed drivers in town. Using these statistics, how many people must be contacted?

Licensed drivers 8,000
Physicians 750
Physicians with drivers licenses 750

Problem Solution

Step 1. Seven hundred and fifty licensed drivers are physicians.
Licensed drivers 8,000, Physicians 750

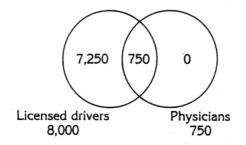

Step 2. 8,000 people need to be contacted.

Problem 28

The government wants to contact all druggists, all gun store owners, and all parents in a town. How many people must be contacted, using these statistics?

Druggists 10
Gun store owners. 5
Parents 3,000
Druggists who own gun stores. 0
Druggists who are parents 7
Gun store owners who are parents 3

Hint: Use this Venn diagram. Note that since no druggists own gun stores, two sections have zeroes.

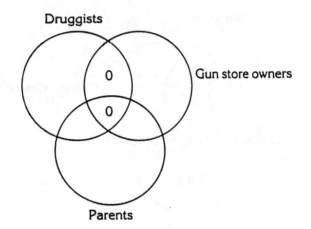

Original Problem

The government wants to contact all druggists, all gun store owners, and all parents in a town. How many people must be contacted, using these statistics?

Druggists   10
Gun store owners.   5
Parents. 3,000
Druggists who own gun stores   0
Druggists who are parents.   7
Gun store owners who are parents   3

Problem Solution

Step 1. The diagram shows the number of people in each category.

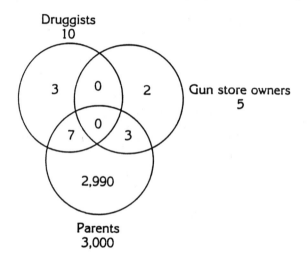

Step 2. The total number that must be contacted is:

$$
\begin{array}{r}
2{,}990 \\
7 \\
3 \\
2 \\
+\quad 3 \\
\hline
3{,}005
\end{array}
$$

Problem 29

If deleting the letters B, R, and A from the word *burglary* leaves a meaningful 3-letter word, circle the first R in this word *burglary*. Otherwise circle the U in the word *burglary* where the word appears for the third time in the exercise.

Original Problem

If deleting the letters B, R, and A from the word *burglary* leaves a meaningful 3-letter word, circle the first R in this word *burglary*. Otherwise circle the U in the word *b(U)rglary* where the word appears for the third time in the exercise.

Problem Solution

Step 1. If deleting the letters B, R, and A from the word burglary . . .

burglary

Step 2. . . . leaves a meaningful 3-letter word . . .

No. The word which remains is *ugly*, and it has four letters.

Step 3. . . . circle the first R in this word *burglary*.

So this should not be done.

Step 4. Otherwise circle the U in the word *burglary* where the word appears for the third time in the exercise.

The word *burglary* occurs for the third time in the last sentence of the problem. The U has been circled on the original problem above.

Problem 30

Indicate the position of the letter in the word *enrage* which is the seventh letter in the alphabet.

    a. First
    b. Second
    c. Third
    d. Fourth
    e. Fifth
    f. Sixth
    g. Seventh
    h. Eighth

Original Problem

Indicate the position of the letter in the word *enrage* which is the seventh letter in the alphabet.

a. First

b. Second

c. Third

d. Fourth

e. Fifth

f. Sixth

g. Seventh

h. Eighth

Problem Solution

Step 1. The seventh letter in the alphabet is: A B C D E F G̲.

Step 2. The letter G is the fifth letter in the word *enrage:* enrage.
                                                                    ↑

Step 3. The word *fifth* is circled above.

Problem 31

What number is twice the distance below 20 as 7 is above 4? Circle your answer below.

27   26   25   23   22   18   17   15   14   13

Original Problem

What number is twice the distance below 20 as 7 is above 4? Circle your answer below.

27   26   25   23   22   18   17   15   (14)   13

Problem Solution

Step 1. The distance that 7 is from 4 is: 7 − 4 = 3.

Step 2. Twice this distance is: 2 × 3 = 6.

Step 3. The number that is 6 below 20 is: 20 − 6 = 14.

The number *14* is circled in the original problem above.

Problem 32

If the fourth number is greater than the second number, circle the third number unless the third number is greater than the fifth number. In this case, circle the number which is the difference between the second number and the seventh number.

8   4   6   5   2   1   9

Original Problem

If the fourth number is greater than the second number, circle the third number unless the third number is greater than the fifth number. In this case, circle the number which is the difference between the second number and the seventh number.

8   4   6   (5)   2   1   9

Problem Solution

Step 1. If the fourth number is greater than the second number . . .

The fourth number is 5. The second number is 4. So the fourth number is greater than the second number.

Step 2. . . . circle the third number unless the third number is greater than the fifth number.

The third number is 6. The fifth number is 2. So the third number is greater than the fifth number and, therefore, it should not be circled.

Step 3. In this case, circle the number which is the difference between the second number and the seventh number.

The second number is 4. The seventh number is 9. The difference between 9 and 4 is 5. Therefore the 5 has been circled on the original problem above.

Problem 33

If the difference between the second and the fourth numbers is greater than the difference between the third and the fifth numbers, circle the seventh number. Otherwise, obtain the difference between the differences and circle it.

3   3   4   6   9   7   9   2

Original Problem

If the difference between the second and the fourth numbers is greater than the difference between the third and the fifth numbers, circle the seventh number. Otherwise, obtain the difference between the differences and circle it.

$$3 \quad 3 \quad 4 \quad 6 \quad 9 \quad 7 \quad 9 \quad \boxed{2}$$

Problem Solution

Step 1. If the difference between the second and the fourth number . . .

The second number is 3. The fourth number is 6. The difference is 3.

Step 2. . . . is greater than the difference between the third and fifth numbers . . .

The third number is 4. The fifth number is 9. The difference is 5.

Therefore, the difference between the second and fourth numbers is not greater than the difference between the third and the fifth number.

Step 3. . . . circle the seventh number.

This should not be done.

Step 4. Otherwise, obtain the *difference between the differences* and circle it.

The 2 differences are 3 and 5. The difference between these two numbers is 2. Therefore, the difference between the differences is 2.

The *2* has been circled on the original problem above.

Problem 34

Circle the letter in the name *Anthony* which is 3 letters before the letter that follows the middle letter of the name.

Original Problem

Circle the letter in the name A(n)thony which is 3 letters before the letter that follows the middle letter of the name.

Problem Solution

Step 1. The middle letter in Anthony is *H: Anthony.*

Step 2. The letter which follows *H* is *O: Anthony.*

Step 3. The letter which is 3 letters before *O* is *N: Anthony.*

Therefore *N* has been circled on the original problem above.

Problem 35

Cross out the letter in the word *participate* which is 2 letters before the second *T.*

Original Problem

Cross out the letter in the word *participate* which is 2 letters before the second *T*.

Problem Solution

Step 1. The second *T* in *participate* is the one next to the *E: participate.*

Step 2. Two letters before this *T* is *P: participate.*

This *P* has been crossed out on the original problem above.

Problem 36 A Problem in Code Breaking

In a foreign language *lev klula buj* means "buy green peppers." However, words in this tongue are not always spoken in the same order as in English. For example, *buj* does not mean "peppers." Also, *ajm buj gyst* means "big green cars" and *lkuka lev ajm* means "quickly buy cars." How would you say *big peppers* in this tongue?

Hint: Write all 3 foreign phrases with their English translations next to them, then compare the phrases to see the words they have in common.

    a. *buj klula*   b. klula buj   c. *klula gyst*
    d. *lev gyst*   e. *lkuka ajm*

Original Problem

In a foreign language *leu klula buj* means "buy green peppers." However, words in this tongue are not always spoken in the same order as in English. For example, *buj* does not mean "peppers." Also, *ajm buj gyst* means "big green cars" and *lkuka leu ajm* means "quickly buy cars." How would you say *big peppers* in this tongue?

Hint: Write all 3 foreign phrases with their English translations next to them, then compare the phrases to see the words they have in common.

    a. *buj klula*   b. klula buj   c. *klula gyst*
    d. *leu gyst*   e. *lkuka ajm*

Problem Solution

Step 1. Three phrases are given in both the foreign tongue and English. These are:

    (1) *leu klula buj*—"buy green peppers"
    (2) *ajm buj gyst*—"big green cars"
    (3) *lkuka leu ajm*—"quickly buy cars"

Step 2. The foreign word (1) and (2) have in common is *buj*; the English word they have in common is *green*. So *buj* must mean *green*.

Step 3. Apparently the foreign tongue has a different grammar than English since *green* is the second word in both (1) and (2), but *buj* is not the second word in (1) and (2).

Step 4. The foreign word that (1) and (3) have in common is *leu*; the English word they have in common is *buy*. So *leu* must mean *buy*.

Step 5. The foreign word that (2) and (3) have in common is *ajm*; the English word they have in common is *cars*. So *ajm* must mean *cars*.

Step 6. The problem asks for the translation of "big peppers." The 3 words which have already been translated are:

green—*buj*   buy—*lev*   cars—*ajm*

Step 7. The word *peppers* is contained in (1). Since *lev* and *buj* are already known to be *buy* and *green*, *klula* must be *peppers*.

Step 8. The word *big* is contained in (2). Since *buj* and *ajm* are already known to be *green* and *cars*, *gyst* must be *big*.

klula—*peppers*   *gyst*—*big*

Step 9. Therefore, "big peppers" must have the words *klula* and *gyst*. This is answer c.

Problem 37

In a different language *luk eir lail* means "heavy little package," *bo lail* means "heavy man," and *luk jo* means "pretty package." How would you say "little man" in this language?

Original Problem

In a different language *luk eir lail* means "heavy little package," *bo lail* means "heavy man," and *luk jo* means "pretty package." How would you say "little man" in this language?

Problem Solution

Step 1. *Luk eir lail* means "heavy little package;" *bo lail* means "heavy man."

The foreign word the 2 phrases have in common is *lail*; the English word they have in common is *heavy*. So apparently *lail* means *heavy*.

Step 2. The phrase *bo lail* means "heavy man," and since *lail* means *heavy*, *bo* must mean *man*.

Step 3. *Luk eir lail* means "heavy little package;" *luk jo* means "pretty package."

The foreign word they have in common is *luk*; the English word they have in common is *package*. So *luk* must mean *package*.

Step 4. *Luk eir lail* means "heavy little package." Since *luk* means *package*, and *lail* means *heavy*, *eir* must mean *little*.

Step 5. How would you say "little man" in this language?

It has been determined that: *Bo* means *man*; *Eir* means *little*.

Step 6. The foreign language apparently expresses certain ideas in the reverse order of English—adjectives follow nouns.

Therefore, "little man" is: *bo eir*.

Problem 38

José owes Som $27.00. Som owes Fred $6.00 and Albert $15.30. If, with Som's permission, José pays off Som's debt to Albert, how much does he still owe Som?

Original Problem

> José owes Som $27.00. Som owes Fred $6.00 and Albert $15.30. If, with Som's permission, José pays off Som's debt to Albert, how much does he still owe Som?

Problem Solution

Step 1. The diagram below shows who owes whom money. The arrows point in the direction in which the money is owed.

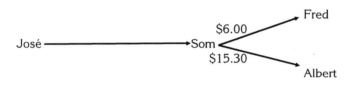

Step 2. José pays off Som's debt to Albert, so this is subtracted from the amount he owes Som.

$$\begin{array}{r} \$27.00 \\ -\ 15.30 \\ \hline \$11.70 \end{array}$$

Step 3. José still owes Som $11.70.

Problem 39

Sally loaned $7.00 to Betty. But Sally borrowed $15.00 from Estella and $32.00 from Joan. Moreover, Joan owes $3.00 to Estella and $7.00 to Betty. One day the women got together at Betty's house to straighten out their accounts. Which woman left with $18.00 more than she came with?

Hint: On your diagram, use arrows to show which person has to return money to which other person. Show the direction in which the money must be returned.

Original Problem

Sally loaned $7.00 to Betty. But Sally borrowed $15.00 from Estella and $32.00 from Joan. Moreover, Joan owes $3.00 to Estella and $7.00 to Betty. One day the women got together at Betty's house to straighten out their accounts. Which woman left with $18.00 more than she came with?

Problem Solution

Step 1. The problem began "Sally loaned $7.00 to Betty." This is shown below with the arrow indicating the direction to which the money must be returned.

$$\text{Sally} \xleftarrow{\quad \$7.00 \quad} \text{Betty}$$

Step 2. The entire pattern of debts is shown in the following diagram.

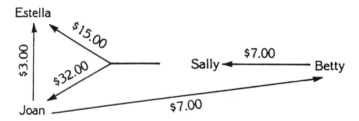

Step 3. Which girl left with $18.00 more than she came with?

The diagram shows that Estella received $3.00 from Joan and $15.00 from Sally, for a total of $18.00.

Estella left with $18.00 more than she came with.

Problem 40

Lester has 12 times as many marbles as Kathy. John has half as many as Judy. Judy has half as many as Lester. Kathy has 6 marbles. How many marbles each do Lester and John have? You do not need to use algebra to solve this problem.

Original Problem

> Lester has 12 times as many marbles as Kathy. John has half as many as Judy. Judy has half as many as Lester. Kathy has 6 marbles. How many marbles each do Lester and John have?

Problem Solution

Step 1. Kathy has 6 marbles.

Step 2. Lester has 12 times as many marbles as Kathy. So Lester has 72 (12 × 6) marbles.

In mathematical shorthand this can be written:

> Lester's marbles = 12 × Kathy's marbles
> Lester's marbles = 12 × 6
> Lester's marbles = 72

Step 3. Judy has half as many as Lester. So Judy has ½ of 72 = 36.

This can be written:

> Judy's marbles = ½ × Lester's marbles
> Judy's marbles = ½ × 72
> Judy's marbles = 36

Step 4. John has half as many as Judy. So John has ½ of 36 = 18.

Step 5. Lester has 72 marbles; John has 18.

ADDITIONAL PROBLEMS

1. Betty is shorter than Sally. Cynthia is taller than Sally. Carla is shorter than Betty. Is Sally shorter or taller than Carla?

2. John is faster than Pete. Dave is faster than Harvey. Dave is slower than Pete. Which man is fastest and which is slowest?

3. If Bob and Fred are both taller than Tom, while Hal is taller than Bob but shorter than Fred, which man is tallest and which is second tallest?

4. Gladys is a teacher, Sally a truck driver, Violet a crane operator, and Hannah a Hollywood stuntwoman. The truck driver is heavier than Hannah. The crane operator is lighter than the stuntwoman. Gladys is heavier than the truck driver. Which woman is heaviest and which is lightest?

5. Dracula hates daylight more than Wolfman unless Frankenstein hates daylight more than Dracula. In that case Wolfman hates daylight more than Dracula but less than Mummy. Mummy hates daylight more than Dracula but less than Frankenstein. Show a diagram of the monsters ordered according to their hatred of daylight.

6. A graph breaking down the cost of education for the state showed that the category labeled "operation, maintenance, and auxiliary agencies" took a greater portion of the budget than "capital outlay." The category labeled "instruction" had the highest portion of the budget, while "interest" had a smaller portion than "capital outlay" and "general control" had a smaller portion than "interest." Show a diagram of the categories ordered according to their portion of the budget.

7. The Great Lakes differ in both their areas (measured in square miles) and their depths. However these two dimensions do not keep step perfectly. For example, Lake Michigan is exceeded in depth only by Lake Superior, but it is exceeded in area by both Lakes Superior and Huron. Lake Superior is by far the largest and deepest of the Great Lakes, but Lake Ontario, which is the smallest in area, is deeper than both Lakes Huron and Erie. Lake Erie is larger than Lake Ontario but it is not only shallower than Huron, it is also shallower than Ontario. Show the order of the Great Lakes according to depth.

8. Bob, Juanita, Ted, and Aretha together have a total income of $1,100 a week, of which $210 is made by Bob. Bob and Juanita together make $500 a week, while Bob and Ted together make $530. How much do Juanita and Aretha make together?

9. Three women—Pat, Joan, and Mary—have between them a total of 30 dresses of which 15 are cotton and the rest are either wool or synthetic fibre. Pat has 3 cotton dresses and 3 synthetics. Mary, who has a total of 8 dresses, has 4 cotton dresses. Pat has the same number of wool dresses as Mary has cotton dresses. Joan has as many wool dresses as Pat has cotton dresses. And Mary also has as many wool dresses as Pat has cotton dresses. How many total dresses does Joan have? (Show the table completely filled in.)

10. Four lawn care fanatics, Fred, John, Alice, and Nina between them own 86 grass cutting devices consisting of shears, string trimmers, and power mowers. Fred likes to be close to his work, so he owns 8 shears and 13 string trimmers, but no mower. John is just the opposite. He prefers to stay as far from the work as possible and therefore owns only power mowers, 33 in all! Alice is an all-around gardener who owns 5 shears, 8 power mowers, and various string trimmers. Nina, a woman of many talents, has a total of 15 implements, among which are 3 shears and 5 string trimmers. Interestingly, the four fanatics own more than twice as many mowers as string trimmers, 48 mowers in all. How many string trimmers does Alice own?

11. In this problem the "first quarter of the year" means January, February, and March. The "second quarter" is April, May, and June, and so on.

Acme Realtors sold 23 houses during the first quarter of the year and again during the last quarter. Sales during the middle two quarters were not quite as good, so that the annual sales total was 57 houses. B & B Realty company sold 50 houses during the second quarter and half that many during the fourth quarter, for a total annual sales of 75 houses. Arco sold as many houses during the third quarter as B & B sold during the entire year, but during the other three quarters they did no better than B & B during the first quarter. Together the three companies sold 79 houses during the third quarter. How many total houses did the three companies sell during the second quarter?

12. John, Harry, and Phil are married to Sally, Nancy, and Arlene, but not necessarily in that order. John, who is Sally's brother, has five children. Nancy, who is a certified public accountant, wants to wait several years

before starting a family. Harry is married to John's sister. Who is Phil married to?

13. Judy, Celia, and Betty are a math teacher, a truck driver, and a housewife, but not necessarily in that order. Judy can't drive and is married to the brother of the math teacher. Celia is the best friend of the truck driver. Betty had a bad experience with math in grade school and has avoided all contact with math since then. What is each woman's occupation?

14. At Ajax Plastics the shipping clerk, the stockgirl, the saleswoman, and the cashier are Rose, Hannah, Geraldine, and Mary Jo, but Mr. Bigwig, the president of Ajax, can't remember who is which. Bigwig does, however, know these facts: Hannah likes both the saleswoman and the cashier; Mary Jo rides to work with the saleswoman and the cashier; the shipping clerk comes to work alone; Rose is slightly jealous of the cashier. Match up the women with their occupations.

15. You are facing south. You turn left, make an about-face, turn right, and turn right again. Which direction is behind you?

16. You are facing northeast and make an about-face. Which direction is on your right?

17. A man went to bed at 10:25 P.M. and arose at 4:10 A.M. How long was he in bed?

18. In Boontown streets that begin with a vowel run east-west unless they also end in a vowel in which case they run north-south. Other streets can go either way. Berkeley street is perpendicular to Alice street. In which direction does Berkeley run?

19. In a city known as the Big Carrot, streets that begin with a vowel and end with a consonant run east-west while those that begin with a consonant and end with a vowel run north-south. Other streets can go either way. A car driving north makes a left turn. Is it now traveling parallel or perpendicular to Eric Street?

20. There is a car traveling north in the Big Carrot, the city described in problem 19. Is the car traveling parallel or perpendicular to Washington Street which is perpendicular to Rose Street?

21. Make a Venn diagram with 3 circles showing these relationships.

    All x are y. Some y are z. No x are z.

22. Make a Venn diagram with 3 circles showing these relationships.

    All x are y. Some z are x. Some z are not y. Some z are y but not x.

23. Make a Venn diagram with 4 circles showing these relationships.

    All x are y. No y are w. All v are w.

24. Make a Venn diagram showing the relationships among animals, birds, and ducks, using one circle to represent animals, another for birds, and a third for ducks.

25. Make a Venn diagram showing the relationships among animals, brown animals, and dogs, using one circle to represent animals, another for brown animals, and a third for dogs.

26. On Halloween the Big Pumpkin visits the homes of all children, all grandmothers, and all poets in town. How many homes does he visit, using these statistics? Draw a Venn diagram.

    Homes with:

Children	800
Grandmothers	250
Poets	60
Children and grandmothers	100
Children and poets	10
Grandmothers and poets	3
Grandmothers and poets and children	1

27. A politician claims that all Catholics and all homeowners in town will vote for him. How many votes does he claim, using these statistics? Draw a Venn diagram.

    Catholics.......................... 400
    Homeowners...................... 1200
    Catholic homeowners 300

For the next four problems, assume the first two statements are correct and make a diagram to represent the relationships. Then answer the questions.

28. All crabs are birds. Some birds are blue.

    a. Can you be certain that all crabs are blue?

    b. Can you be certain that some crabs are blue?

29. Some elephants are lions. All lions have three eyes.

    a. Can you be certain that all elephants have three eyes?

    b. Can you be certain that some elephants have three eyes?

30. All rifles are automobiles. No automobiles are machines.

    a. Can you be certain that some rifles are machines?

    b. Can you be certain that no rifles are machines?

31. Some paper is white. No white things are usable things.

    a. Can you be certain some paper is usable?

    b. Can you be certain that some paper is not usable?

32. Cross out the letter in the word *fireplace* which is two letters before the letter that precedes the *l*.

33. If the second half of the second name of our first president contains the second letter in *cheese*, circle the second word in this sentence. Otherwise, circle the first word in this sentence.

34. If deleting the first, third, fifth, and seventh letters in the word *education* leaves four more consonants than vowels, circle the first comma in this sentence. Otherwise, circle the second comma.

35. Cross out the letter in the name Jonathan which is two letters after the letter that precedes the *h*.

36. If the fifth letter in the word *sanctuary* is the 18th letter in the alphabet, circle it. Otherwise, circle the letter (in the word) which is the fourteenth letter of the alphabet.

37. *8 9 7 5 3 9 9 2 4 6.* If the sum of the second and the sixth numbers is greater than 14, circle the third number, unless the sum of the second and the sixth numbers is greater than 15, in which case circle the number which is one-half the last number in the series.

38. *9 8 7 6 5 4 3 2 1.* Take the difference between the first number and the sixth number. Write the difference here _____. Now take the difference between the fifth number and the seventh number. Write it here _____. Finally, take the difference between these two differences and write it here _____.

39. *8 2 7 5 6 4 5 3 4.* If the difference between the first number and the fifth number is greater than the difference between the first number and the sixth number circle the seven. Otherwise take the difference between the differences and circle it.

40. *1 2 4 7 4 5 3.* Subtract the third number from double the fifth number unless double the fourth number is more than the sum of the sixth and seventh numbers; in this case subtract the second number from double the sixth number. Then add two unless the third number is more than the sixth number in which case subtract one. Circle your answer below.

     a. 9   *b.* 5   *c.* 10   *d.* 2   *e.* 7   *f.* 6   *g.* 1   *h.* 11

41. In a foreign language *ho lew gi* means "buy every dog," *lew ra* means "dog food," and *gi trj nk* means "every green car." Which words would you use to say "every food"? (Ignore the order of the words in answering the question.)

42. In a different language *si gumba lo* means "not very sweet," *ja lo* means "not brown," and *ba ja gumba* means "very brown coffee." How would you say "sweet coffee" in this language?

    a. *lo gumba*   b. *ja gumba*   c. *ba si*   d. *gumba ba*   e. *ja si*

43. In 1968 the Detroit Tigers beat the St. Louis Cardinals in the World Series. Mickey Lolich pitched two winning games for Detroit. In 1946 the Red Sox won the pennant, but were beaten by the Cardinals in the World Series. Country Slaughter was the Cardinals' hero. Twelve years before that, the Cardinals beat the Tigers in the Series. Dizzy Dean was the pitching hero. Four years before they beat the Red Sox and 8 years after they beat Detroit, the Cardinals beat the New York Yankees. The next year they lost to the Yankees, but the following year they beat the St. Louis Browns, now known as the Baltimore Orioles. Twenty-one years after they beat the Red Sox, they beat them again and 22 years after they beat the Yankees, they beat them again. Eighteen years after this win over the Yankees, the Cardinals took the Series from the Milwaukee Brewers. List the dates of the Series played by the Cardinals, along with the winners and losers. Include the hero or pitching star when one is mentioned.*

*This problem was contributed by William Hart, Jr., a teacher at Balboa High School in San Francisco. For additional contributed problems see our web site at: www.whimbey.com

Awareness and Communication of Thinking

Now that you have worked a number of problems aloud, you may be more aware of the mental steps you use to solve problems and also better able to explain the steps. Rate your progress on the diagram below.

Awareness

Compared to when you began this chapter, how aware are you of the process you use to solve problems. Mark your assessment with an "X."

0	1	2	3	4	5	6	7	8	9	10

Not more aware and not better at explaining mental steps

A little more aware and better at explaining mental steps

Much more aware and better at explaining mental steps

The various exercises in the remaining chapters provide additional opportunities for growing more aware of your thinking activities so you can become a better problem solver and can explain your reasoning to others.

V. SIX MYTHS ABOUT READING

When you read textbooks and other technical material for full comprehension, you must read as carefully as you read the word problems in the last chapter. Occasionally you may not have time to read carefully and you may just skim the material. But you should recognize that when you skim, you will not comprehend many of the details. You cannot learn mathematics by skimming a math text, nor can you learn chemistry, physics, biology, or any other science by skimming textbooks in those areas.

There is a great deal of misinformation about reading. Here are six popular myths about reading which research has shown to be false.

Myth 1. Don't Subvocalize When You Read

You sometimes hear the advice that you should not move your lips, tongue or throat muscles when you read. You should not even hear the words in your mind when you read. You should be a totally "visual" reader. In some books, teachers have been advised to give young pupils candy or gum to prevent subvocalizing, and if necessary to even put a pencil or a ruler in a child's mouth to save him from this habit.

A series of studies have now shown that subvocalizing is useful and perhaps even necessary for good comprehension of difficult material. For example, in one experiment college students who were taught to suppress their subvocalizing responses were only able to maintain good comprehension for easy reading material. Their comprehension of difficult reading material suffered drastically when they didn't subvocalize as they read.

All the evidence indicates that you should subvocalize freely when you read. It can produce better comprehension of technical material and a fuller appreciation of literary writing where alliteration and other poetic devices depend on hearing the words.

Myth 2. Read Only the Key Words

This advice is completely illogical. How can you know which words are the key words, until you first read the words? The advice assumes you have some magical, subliminal mechanism which allows you to pre-read the words and select out the key words which you will then read.

When students do try to read just key words, they frequently emerge with a misinterpretation of the material. For example, one student I worked with read the following sentence silently:

> Some scraps of evidence bear out those who hold a very high opinion of the average level of culture among the Athenians of the Great Age.

I asked the student what the sentence said and he replied: "The level of Greek culture was very high." I said: "How about the first part of the sentence—some scraps of evidence?" He answered that he had skipped over that part and had tried to read just the key words, namely, "high . . . level of culture . . . Athenians."

Myth 3. Don't Be a Word-By-Word Reader

Emerald Dechant, a prominent reading researcher, made the following comments on this myth in the *Eleventh Yearbook of the National Reading Conference:*

> For years, and in many textbooks today, teachers have been and are being urged to teach the child to read two and three words per fixation. However, the best studies show that even college students rarely read more than one word per fixation. The assumption that children could, or at least normally would, recognize such large units, was based on misinterpretations of tachistoscopic research and resulted from a misunderstanding of the basic differences between tachistoscopic and normal reading. The limiting factor in recognition is the mind rather than the eye.[1]

Myth 4. Read in Thought Groups

This myth is closely related to myth 3. Since good readers basically read one word at a time, they obviously do not read in thought groups.

Naturally in reading you group words together mentally. Verbs and prepositions link nouns with other nouns, and so on. But you cannot "read in thought groups" in the sense of visually focussing on groups of words which form thoughts. In fact, this would be logically impossible. You couldn't know

---

[1]Emerald Dechant, "Misinterpretations of Theory and/or Research Lead to Errors in Practice." In *Eleventh Yearbook of the National Reading Conference,* Emery P. Bliesmer and Ralph C. Staiger, editors, Milwaukee, WI: The National Reading Conference, Inc., 1962, page 127.

which words formed a "thought group" until you first read the words. It would be impossible to read by moving your eyes from one thought group to another.

Myth 5. You Can Read at Speeds of 1,000 or More Words a Minute—Without Any Loss of Comprehension

Speed reading "experts" say if you read 250–300 words a minute you are plodding along at a horse-and-buggy rate and wasting your time. You should be reading three to ten times that fast. However, a sample of University of Michigan professors was found to read at an average rate of 303 words per minute, and the average rate for Harvard freshmen was 300 words per minute. Furthermore, a number of experiments have found that when people who have learned to skim at 600 words a minute or more cut back to 300 words per minute their comprehension improves. In study after study, approximately 300 words per minute has turned out to be the maximum rate at which people can read without sacrificing comprehension.

Students preparing for tests like the SAT, GRE, or LSAT can rest assured that a reading speed of 250–300 words a minute will allow them to attain a very high score if their comprehension is strong. Their preparation should consist mainly of strengthening their vocabulary and comprehension skills, not attempting to whip-up their reading speed.

Myth 6. Don't Regress or Re-read

Speed reading "experts" say you should never regress or re-read a section of material, even if you feel you have not understood it well. Re-reading is said to be a bad reading habit and totally unproductive. Instead you should forge ahead and your understanding will be clarified as you read on.

Studies show that good readers do not follow this advice. With textbooks and other complicated material they must frequently re-read sentences and paragraphs to get the full meaning.

A Speed Reading "Guarantee"

One of the major speed reading companies supports its claim by offering to return a portion of your payment if they fail to triple your "reading efficiency." This sounds impressive to many people because they don't know what their "reading efficiency" represents. Here is the definition of reading efficiency:

Reading Efficiency = % Comprehension × Reading Speed

Assume you begin the speed reading course as a good reader who reads at 300 words per minute and answers 95% of the questions correctly on the comprehension test. Your reading efficiency is calculated like this:

$$\text{Reading Efficiency} = 95\% \times 300$$
$$= 285$$

You then complete the speed reading course. Suppose on the test to determine your new reading efficiency you read 2,000 words a minute with 55% comprehension. Your new reading efficiency is calculated to be:

$$\text{Reading Efficiency} = 55\% \times 2,000$$
$$= 1,100$$

Your reading efficiency has more than tripled. But what good is a reading efficiency of 1,100 if it is based on a comprehension score of 55%? Would you want a surgeon to operate on you with anything less than his maximum possible comprehension of medical texts? Don't lawyers, nuclear engineers, and auto mechanics require the maximum possible comprehension to do the best possible job?

If you want to master your academic subjects and perform well on tests, you must read with care and thoroughness, and give the work the time it requires. There are no magical shortcuts. In reading textbooks and technical material, use all the activities of good problem solvers described in chapter III.

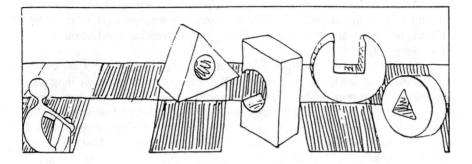

VI. ANALOGIES

Section 1 Introduction

We often explain and emphasize our ideas by using analogies. For example, when we say "John is a chip off the old block," we bring home forcefully the similarity between John and his father. In effect we are saying John is so similar to his father, it's as if John were cut from the same material. Similarly, we read in the Bible "The Lord is my shepherd"—and from just these five words we get a clearer feeling for the protection and comfort felt by the Psalmist than we might from a lengthy, literal essay. Biologists tell us "the heart is like a mechanical pump," and we immediately understand the heart's role in circulating the blood. And in physics, new insights were gained when Lord Rutherford suggested that the solar system be used as a model for the atom, with electrons around the nucleus taken as analogous to planets around the sun.

Each of these statements or comparisons originates in *analogous* thinking. This is shown by presenting each of the ideas in the basic form of the simple analogy.

> John is similar to his father as a chip is similar to the block from which it is cut.
>
> The Lord cares for me as a shepherd cares for his sheep.
>
> The heart moves the blood as a mechanical pump moves fluids.
>
> Electrons circle an atom's nucleus as planets circle the sun.

Analogies help us explain ideas to other people. More than that, they often lead us to new discoveries and inventions. Alexander Graham Bell believed that an apparatus for transmitting human conversation—a telephone—could be constructed. But he had enormous difficulty perfecting a means for converting voice sounds to electrical impulse so that speech could be carried through wires.

143

At one point he tried attaching a harp to an electromagnet. Striking a tuning fork in the vicinity of the harp caused selected strings to resonate, producing electrical waves. But this ponderous contraption was unsatisfactory for conversation.

Bell's friend—the prominent Boston aurist, Dr. Clarence Blake—suggested that Bell study the human ear rather than continue experimenting with mechanical instruments, and gave the inventor an ear with connecting organs cut from the head of a cadaver. Bell observed that although the eardrum was extremely thin and light, it was able to move the three heavy inner-ear bones which formed the mechanical linkage of the ear. Bell later recalled, "it struck me that the bones of the human ear were very massive, indeed, as compared with the delicate thin membrane that operated them, and the thought occurred that if a membrane so delicate could move bones relatively so massive, why should not a thicker and stouter piece of membrane move my piece of steel."

That was the breakthrough. Various iron disks and membranes were tried. Finally in 1875 a diaphragm of gold-beater's skin (which is very thin) was fastened to a metal armature adjacent to an electromagnet and the first working microphone, an integral part of any telephone, was created.

This bit of history is an example of a *biological analogy* furnishing critical information for a mechanical invention. The analogy can be expressed:

Eardrum functions in the ear as diaphragm functions in the telephone.

The strategy of looking for biological analogies to aid in technological developments is so fruitful that an entirely new science called Bionics has come into existence. The *Journal of Creative Behavior* describes Bionics in the following way:

Bionics is a new approach to system design. It is the study of the structure, function, and mechanisms of plants and animals to gain design information for analogous man-made systems.[1]

The primary role which analogous thinking plays in scientific invention, mathematical induction, and literary creation indicates that when a person systematically analyzes an analogy he uses the same mental skills that are important in comprehending and integrating all areas of advanced human knowledge. As you work the analogy problems in the chapter, you will find it necessary to spell ideas out fully, formulate precise relationships of facts, seek correspondences between diverse ideas, and compare relationships for similarities and differences. These are the activities which underlie the mastery of all academic courses, stretching from poetry to political science to calculus. These are the mental tools which have been used to shape all cultural and technological achievements.

---

[1]"Bionics," *Journal of Creative Behavior.* Vol. 2, No. 1, Winter, 1967. p. 52–57.

Section 2 The "Relationship Sentence"

Here is an analogy:

Gills are related to *fish* as *lungs* are related to *humans.*

To really understand this analogy you must be able to show that the relationship between gills and fish is in some way the same as the relationship between lungs and humans. You must be able to spell out exactly what the relationship is.

Gills are used for breathing by *fish.*
Lungs are used for breathing by *humans.*

You could show the relationship with a "Relationship Sentence" like this:

Relationship Sentence: _____ are used for breathing by _____.

Section 3 Choosing Relationship Sentences

Each of the following problems presents an analogy and three possible relationship sentences. Your task is to pick the correct relationship sentence and substitute both pairs of words into the sentence to show it is correct.

Example 1

Carpenter is to *saw* as *plumber* is to *wrench.*

Relationship Sentence a. A _____ is a _____.
Relationship Sentence b. A _____ cuts wood with a _____.
Relationship Sentence c. A _____ uses a tool called a _____.

Which relationship sentence is correct? Let's try substituting both pairs of words in relationship sentence a.

Relationship Sentence a. A *carpenter* is a *saw.*
A *plumber* is a *wrench.*

This is wrong. A carpenter is not a saw and a plumber is not a wrench.
Let's try relationship sentence b.

Relationship Sentence b. A *carpenter* cuts wood with a *saw.*
A *plumber* cuts wood with a *wrench.*

This is wrong. A plumber does not cut wood with a wrench.
Finally we'll try relationship sentence c.

Relationship Sentence c. A *carpenter* uses a tool called a *saw*.
A *plumber* uses a tool called a *wrench*.

This is a good relationship sentence. It shows why we say the relationship between carpenter and saw is similar to the relationship between plumber and wrench.

One more example is presented below.

Example 2

Choose the correct relationship sentence. Then copy it twice; once with stewardess-airplane substituted into the blanks and the second time with waitress-restaurant in the blanks.

Stewardess is to *airplane* as *waitress* is to *restaurant*.

Relationship Sentence a. A _____ gives safety instructions in a(n) _____.

Relationship Sentence b. A _____ works in a(n) _____.

Relationship Sentence c. A _____ is a(n) _____.

Solution

The correct answer is relationship sentence b.

I. first word pair: A *stewardess* works in an *airplane*.
II. second word pair: A *waitress* works in a *restaurant*.

There is one complication. You say "an" airplane, but you say "a" restaurant. Because of this, the *n* is put in parenthesis in the relationship sentence.

A _____ works in a(n) _____.

The parenthesis means that the *n* can be either used or omitted, whichever is appropriate.

ANALOGY PROBLEMS

For each of the following analogies, pick the best relationship sentence. Then copy that relationship sentence twice, once with the first word pair placed in the blanks, and once with the second word pair. Include or omit any letters in parentheses as appropriate.

Here is an example.

book is to *paper* as *shirt* is to *cloth*

    a. A _____ is made of linen or some other _____.

    b. A _____ is words printed on _____.

    c. A _____ is primarily made of _____.

Sentence c is correct.

    I. first word pair: A *book* is primarily made of *paper.*

    II. second word pair: A *shirt* is primarily made of *cloth.*

1. *guitar* is to *pick* as *fiddle* is to *bow*

    a. A _____ is played with a _____.

    b. A _____ is plucked with a _____.

    c. A _____ is a _____.

    I. first word pair:

    II. second word pair:

2. *water* is to *thirsty* as *food* is to *hungry*

    a. You drink _____ when you are _____.

    b. You drink _____ and eat _____.

    c. You consume _____ when you are _____.

    I. first word pair:

    II. second word pair:

3. *bicycle* is to *airplane* as *cabin* is to *skyscraper*

    a. A _____ and a(n) _____ are used for travel.

    b. A _____ is simpler but used for the same purpose as a(n) _____.

    c. You can live in a _____ or a(n) _____.

    I. first word pair:

    II. second word pair:

4. *hotter* is to *hot* as *colder* is to *cold*

    a. _____ means the same as _____.

    b. _____ means to _____.

    c. _____ means more _____.

    I. first word pair:

    II. second word pair:

5. *decrease* is to *smaller* as *magnify* is to *larger*

   a. _____ means _____.

   b. _____ means make _____.

   c. _____ means make shorter or _____.

   I. first word pair:

   II. second word pair:

6. *student* is to *truant* as *soldier* is to *A.W.O.L.*

   a. A _____ out of school is _____.

   b. A _____ can be court marshalled for being _____.

   c. A _____ who is absent illegally is _____.

   I. first word pair:

   II. second word pair:

7. *polluted* is to *pure* as *tainted* is to *undefiled*

   a. _____ and _____ start with the same letter.

   b. _____ and _____ are opposite in meaning.

   c. _____ and _____ mean dirty.

   I. first word pair:

   II. second word pair:

8. *dam* is to *flood* as *vaccination* is to *disease*

    a. A _____ holds back water to prevent a _____.

    b. A _____ is given by a doctor to prevent a _____.

    c. A _____ is used to prevent a _____.

    I. first word pair:

    II. second word pair:

9. *fence* is to *garden* as *bumper* is to *car*

    a. A _____ helps protect a _____.

    b. A _____ keeps trespassers out of a _____.

    c. A _____ surrounds a _____.

    I. first word pair:

    II. second word pair:

10. *speed* is to *injured* as *caution* is to *safe*

    a. _____ may result in a person being _____.

    b. _____ and inattention result in a person being _____.

    c. _____ and alertness result in a person being _____.

    I. first word pair:

    II. second word pair:

11. *20* is related to *10* as *50* is related to *25*

    a. _____ is ten more than _____.

    b. _____ is twice _____.

    c. _____ is one-half of _____.

    I. first word pair:

    II. second word pair:

12. *20* is related to *10* as *50* is related to *40*

    a. _____ is ten more than _____.

    b. _____ is twice _____.

    c. _____ is one-half of _____.

    I. first word pair:

    II. second word pair:

13. *50* is related to *48* as *67* is related to *64*

    a. _____ is two more than _____.

    b. _____ is larger than _____.

    c. _____ is smaller than _____.

    I. first word pair:

    II. second word pair:

14. *30* is related to *20* as *60* is related to *40*

    a. _____ is ten more than _____.

    b. _____ is one and one-half times _____.

    c. _____ is smaller than _____.

    I. first word pair:

    II. second word pair:

15. *20* is related to *40* as *30* is related to *60*

    a. _____ is twice _____.

    b. _____ is larger than _____.

    c. _____ is one-half of _____.

    I. first word pair:

    II. second word pair:

16. *40* is related to *30* as *80* is related to *60*

    a. _____ is three-quarters of _____.

    b. _____ is one and one-third times _____.

    c. _____ is smaller than _____.

    I. first word pair:

    II. second word pair:

17. *50* is related to *60* as *10* is related to *12*

    a. _____ is 10 less than _____.

    b. _____ is one and one-fifth times _____.

    c. _____ is five-sixths of _____.

      I. first word pair:

      II. second word pair:

18. *70* is related to *80* as *14* is related to *16*

    a. _____ is eight-sevenths of _____.

    b. _____ is seven-eighths of _____.

    c. _____ is seven-fourteenths of _____.

      I. first word pair:

      II. second word pair:

19. *warm* is to *hot* as *smile* is to *laugh*

    a. (A) _____ is a mild form of (a) _____.

    b. (A) _____ and a _____ stem from something funny.

    c. (A) _____ and (a) _____ are the opposite of cold.

      I. first word pair:

      II. second word pair:

20. *roar* is to *sea* as *howl* is to *wind*

    a. _____ is the sound of water crashing in the _____.

    b. _____ is the sound of the turbulent air of the _____.

    c. _____ is the sound of the _____.

    I. first word pair:

    II. second word pair:

21. *surgeon* is to *scalpel* as *writer* is to *words*

    a. The tool of the _____ is (the) _____.

    b. A _____ performs appendectomies with a _____.

    c. A _____ uses _____ to communicate ideas.

    I. first word pair:

    II. second word pair:

22. *menu* is to *restaurant* as *guidebook* is to *city*

    a. A _____ shows the foods available in a _____.

    b. A _____ lists what is available in a _____.

    c. A _____ lists the sights in a _____.

    I. first word pair:

    II. second word pair:

23. *rake* is to *hoe* as *fork* is to *spoon*

    a. A _____ has prongs while a _____ is solid.

    b. A _____ and a _____ are used in gardening.

    c. A _____ and a _____ are eating utensils.

    I. first word pair:

    II. second word pair:

24. *aspirin* is to *headache* as *solace* is to *misfortune*

    a. _____ is taken with water to relieve a _____.

    b. _____ relieves the pain of a _____.

    c. _____ causes a _____.

    I. first word pair:

    II. second word pair:

When you have completed this series of problems, discuss your answers in class to be sure they are correct.

Homework Assignment

After you have had an opportunity to work some problems in class, make up several problems of the same type for homework. Each problem should include an analogy and three possible relationship sentences, only one of which is correct. Also, show that both pairs of words can be placed into the correct relationship sentence.

VII. WRITING RELATIONSHIP SENTENCES

Section 1 Introduction

The problems in this chapter are very similar to those in the last chapter except that you must write the relationship sentences yourself. Here is an example.

paper is to *trees* as *iron* is to *ore*

A good problem solver who read and thought aloud as she attempted to write a relationship sentence for this analogy responded as follows: "Paper is to trees as iron is to ore. I think you get iron from ore. And I guess you also get paper from trees. So that's the analogy. Paper is produced from trees and iron is produced from ore."

The problem solver wrote her ideas in two separate sentences so that she could see them clearly and compare them. Then she wrote the relationship sentence with blanks.

    Sentence 1. Paper is produced from trees.

    Sentence 2. Iron is produced from ore.

    Relationship Sentence: _____ is produced from _____.

Section 2 Sample Problem

Formulate a relationship sentence which explains why the analogy below holds true. Follow the steps used by the problem solver in the last section.

First write two separate sentences—one sentence showing the relationship between the first pair of words in the analogy, and a second sentence showing the relationship between the second pair of words.

Then write the relationship sentence with blanks to accommodate either pair of words.

If you are using this book in a class, one student should solve the problem aloud and write the sentences on the chalkboard.

mouth is to *talk* as *hand* is to *grasp*

Sentence 1.

Sentence 2.

Relationship Sentence:

Section 3 Solution

Here is the analogy you were presented with in section 2.

mouth is to *talk* as *hand* is to *grasp*

In writing the relationship sentence, you may have begun by saying "A mouth can be used to talk, and a hand can be used to grasp."

A mouth can be used to talk.

A hand can be used to grasp.

Then you might have written the core of these sentences with blanks, allowing either word pair to be substituted correctly.

A _____ can be used to _____.

The relationship sentence that you wrote may have been a little different than this one. For example, here are two equally good variations.

The _____ is used to _____.

A person employs his _____ to _____.

Any relationship sentence which shows why the analogy holds is fine.
In working the problems in this chapter, there is only one restriction to keep in mind. Write the relationship sentence so that the word pairs remain in the same order as they occur in the original analogy. For instance, consider the relationship sentence.

You can _____ with your _____.

Notice that in order to place the word pairs (mouth-talk and hand-grasp) meaningfully into the blanks you must reverse their order. For example, you must change "mouth-talk" to "talk-mouth."

You can talk with your mouth.

You can grasp with your hand.

In working the problems in this chapter, avoid writing relationship sentences which invert word order. Instead, always write the relationship sentence in a way which allows you to place the words into the blanks in the same order that they occurred in the original analogy. This will make it easier to check whether the relationship sentence is totally correct. You will see how important this is in subsequent chapters when you begin analyzing more complex analogies.

Section 4 Examples

Relationship sentences are very much like mathematical equations. For example, consider this number analogy:

6 is related to *2* as *21* is related to *7*

A satisfactory relationship sentence is:

_____ is three times _____.

If you know a little algebra, you will recognize that this relationship sentence is equivalent to the following algebraic equation.

$y = 3x$

This is true because:

$6 = 3(2)$		$6 = 3$ times 2
$21 = 3(7)$	or	$21 = 3$ times 7

A relationship sentence is written in common language (such as standard English)—and can show a connection either between words, or between numbers. On the other hand, an algebraic equation is written in mathematical symbols, and can only show a connection between numbers.

Let's look at a few more facts about number analogies. Consider this one:

70 is related to *30* as *35* is related to *15*

At first sight, it might occur to you that 70 is 40 more than 30, and you might consider writing this relationship sentence:

_____ is 40 more than _____.

But when you check this against the second half of the analogy, you see that 35 is not 40 more than 15. You would then discard your first conclusion, and work your way to the correct relationship.

_____ is 7/3 of _____.

By way of contrast, consider another analogy.

50 is related to *10* as *110* is related to *70*

In this case it is true that for both the first pair of numbers and the second pair of numbers, the difference is 40. With this analogy a good relationship sentence is:

_____ is 40 more than _____.

This relationship sentence can also be written as an algebraic equation:

$$y = x + 40$$

We check it by substituting the numbers from the analogy:

$$50 = 10 + 40$$
$$110 = 70 + 40$$

The close connection between relationship sentences and algebraic equations shows something very important. When you practice writing relationship sentences (with blanks into which either pair of words can be substituted) you are sharpening the same analytical skill that you depend on in understanding and manipulating all algebraic expressions. Strange as it may sound, by practicing verbal analogies you can increase your strength in mathematical problem solving.

Homework Assignment

Make up several analogies. For each analogy write one sentence showing the relationship between the first pair of words, another sentence showing the relationship between the second pair of words, and a relationship sentence.

RELATIONSHIP PROBLEMS

The following problems involve writing relationship sentences for analogies. Work in pairs, and do all your reading and thinking aloud. Also, to guide your thinking and make it more visible to your partner, please use this procedure:

1. Examine the analogy, reading and thinking aloud.

2. When you have discovered the common relationship, write two separate sentences: One sentence using the common relationship and the first pair of words, and another sentence using the common relationship and the second pair of words.

3. As your final step, write the relationship sentence with the blanks—and check that it is entirely correct.

Here is an example:

> *legs* are to *chair* as *wheels* are to *car*

Sentence 1. Legs support a *chair.*

Sentence 2. Wheels support a *car.*

Relationship Sentence: _____ support a _____.

Problems

1. *arrive* is to *depart* as *find* is to *lose*

   Sentence 1.

   Sentence 2.

   Relationship Sentence:

2. *books* are to *library* as *paintings* are to *museum*

   Sentence 1.

   Sentence 2.

   Relationship Sentence:

3. *pen* is to *typewriter* as *horse* is to *automobile*

   Sentence 1.

   Sentence 2.

   Relationship Sentence:

4. *key* is to *typewriter* as *steering wheel* is to *automobile*

   Sentence 1.

   Sentence 2.

   Relationship Sentence:

5. *author* is to *book* as *mother* is to *child*

   Sentence 1.

   Sentence 2.

   Relationship Sentence:

6. *electricity* is to *motor* as *ambition* is to *human*

   Sentence 1.

   Sentence 2.

   Relationship Sentence:

7. *artist* is to *talent* as *athlete* is to *coordination*

   Sentence 1.

   Sentence 2.

   Relationship Sentence:

8. *roots* are to *plant* as *mouth* is to *animal*

   Sentence 1.

   Sentence 2.

   Relationship Sentence:

9. *hand* is to *shoulder* as *foot* is to *hip*

   Sentence 1.

   Sentence 2.

   Relationship Sentence:

10. *peacock* is to *bird* as *tuxedo* is to *suit*

    Sentence 1.

    Sentence 2.

    Relationship Sentence:

11. *verdict* is to *jury* as *sentence* is to *judge*

    Sentence 1.

    Sentence 2.

    Relationship Sentence:

12. *hound* is to *fox* as *lion* is to *zebra*

    Sentence 1.

    Sentence 2.

    Relationship Sentence:

Note: For the next five problems, do not use the relationship sentence "_____
is smaller/larger than _____." Instead, write one which describes the
relationship more fully, such as "_____ is 25 more than _____."

13. *30* is related to *10* as *45* is related to *15*

    Sentence 1.

    Sentence 2.

    Relationship Sentence:

14. *10* is related to *40* as *80* is related to *110*

    Sentence 1.

    Sentence 2.

    Relationship Sentence:

15. *10* is related to *30* as *40* is related to *120*

    Sentence 1.

    Sentence 2.

    Relationship Sentence:

16. *50* is related to *20* as *90* is related to *60*

    Sentence 1.

    Sentence 2.

    Relationship Sentence:

17. *50* is related to *20* as *25* is related to *10*

    Sentence 1.

    Sentence 2.

    Relationship Sentence:

18. *roots* are to *plant* as *foundation* is to *building*

    Sentence 1.

    Sentence 2.

    Relationship Sentence:

19. *earth* is to *sun* as *moon* is to *earth*

    Sentence 1.

    Sentence 2.

    Relationship Sentence:

20. *fishes* are to *school* as *wolves* are to *pack*

    Sentence 1.

    Sentence 2.

    Relationship Sentence:

21. *lamp* is to *light* as *furnace* is to *warmth*

    Sentence 1.

    Sentence 2.

    Relationship Sentence:

22. *warm* is to *hot* as *cool* is to *cold*

    Sentence 1.

    Sentence 2.

    Relationship Sentence:

23. *always* is to *often* as *never* is to *seldom*

    Sentence 1.

    Sentence 2.

    Relationship Sentence:

24. *antidote* is to *poison* as *teacher* is to *ignorance*

    Sentence 1.

    Sentence 2.

    Relationship Sentence:

25. *cube* is to *square* as *cylinder* is to *circle*

    Sentence 1.

    Sentence 2.

    Relationship Sentence:

26. *threat* is to *punch* as *growl* is to *bite*

    Sentence 1.

    Sentence 2.

    Relationship Sentence:

27. *itinerary* is to *trip* as *table of contents* is to *book*

   Sentence 1.

   Sentence 2.

   Relationship Sentence:

28. *horns* are to *gore* as *bombs* are to *level*

   Sentence 1.

   Sentence 2.

   Relationship Sentence:

29. *peninsula* is to *ocean* as *bay* is to *land*

   Sentence 1.

   Sentence 2.

   Relationship Sentence:

30. *idea* is to *action* as *seed* is to *flower*

   Sentence 1.

   Sentence 2.

   Relationship Sentence:

31. *sun* is to *moon* as *bulb* is to *reflector*

    Sentence 1.

    Sentence 2.

    Relationship Sentence:

32. *depressed* is to *economy* as *incapacitated* is to *person*

    Sentence 1.

    Sentence 2.

    Relationship Sentence:

33. *bi* is to *two* as *pent* is to *five*

    Sentence 1.

    Sentence 2.

    Relationship Sentence:

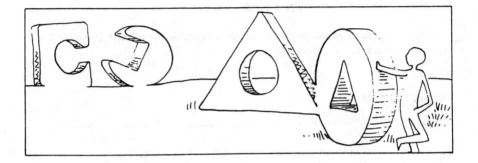

VIII. HOW TO FORM ANALOGIES

Section 1 Introduction

This chapter asks that you solve analogy problems of the type that are included in most IQ tests, job applicant tests, and college-entrance exams such as the College Boards, Gradute Record Exam, and Miller's Analogies Test. Working these problems will help you score higher on such tests. In addition, it will strengthen your analytical skills for all academic work.

Here is a sample problem. Your task is to select the answer which forms the best analogy when the words are placed into the blank. Please work the problem aloud. Read the entire problem aloud, including all the answer choices. For each of the answer choices, explain why it is either correct or incorrect—so the rest of the class understands your reasons for picking one alternative as the best answer.

After you have chosen your answer, write a relationship sentence which shows the rationale underlying the analogy.

thermometer is to *temperature* as _____ is to _____.

        a. telescope : astronomy   *c.* scale : weight
        b. clock : minutes   *d.* microscope : biologist

Relationship Sentence:

Section 2 Problem Solver's Response

Here is how a good problem solver worked the problem presented in section 1. Read the solution aloud.

Original Problem

thermometer is to temperature as _____ is to _____.

      a. telescope : astronomy   *c.* scale : weight
      b. clock : minutes   *d.* microscope : biologist

Problem Solver's Response

The Problem Solver read the relationship sentence, then the four options aloud, considering each one in turn.

"Thermometer is to temperature as *blank* is to *blank*." A thermometer measures temperature.

"Telescope : astronomy." A telescope doesn't measure astronomy.

"Clock : minutes." A clock measures minutes. So this might be a good answer.

"Scale : weight." A scale measures weight. This could also be the answer.

"Microscope : biologist." A microscope doesn't measure a biologist.

It seems as though there are two good answers. Let me go back over them. A thermometer measures temperature, a clock measures minutes, and a scale measures weight. The word "minutes" is different from "temperature" or "weight." A clock measures time, not minutes. Minutes are units of time—just as degrees are units of temperature, and pounds are units of weight.

So the best answer is *c*, scale : weight. Temperature and weight are dimensions. But minutes aren't dimensions; they are units of a dimension. A thermometer measures the dimension temperature, and a scale measures the dimension weight.

Section 3 Sample Problem

In the problem solution in the last section, the problem solver defined the relationship between the first pair of words (he observed that a thermometer measures temperature) and then looked to see if he could find a similar relationship in any of the other word pairs. Use the same approach with this problem. State the relationship which you see in the first pair of words. Then read each of the answer choices aloud and explain why the words do or do not have the same relationship.

horse is to *animal* as _____ is to _____.

      a. cow : milk   *c.* oak : wood
      b. farm : pig   *d.* saddle : stallion

Relationship Sentence:

Section 4 Problem Solver's Response

Here is how a good problem solver worked the problem presented in Section 3. Read the solution aloud.

Original Problem

horse is to *animal* as _____ is to _____.

         a. cow : milk   *c.* oak : wood
         b. farm : pig   *d.* saddle : stallion

Problem Solver's Response

The Problem Solver read the relationship sentence aloud, then considered the four options in turn.	"*Horse* is to *animal* as blank is to blank." A horse is an animal.
	It is a type of animal.
	"*Cow : milk.*" A cow isn't a type of milk . . . it gives milk.
	"*Farm : pig.*" A farm isn't a type of pig.
	"*Oak : wood.*" Oak is a type of wood. So this forms an analogy.
	"*Saddle : stallion.*" A saddle isn't a type of stallion.
	Answer *c* is best. A horse is a type of animal and oak is a type of wood.

Section 5 Sample Problem

A common error in analogy problems is to select an answer which reverses the direction of the relationship. Be careful not to do that in the following problem.

State the relationship between the first two numbers, and then explain why each of the answer choices does or doesn't form an analogy.

2 is to *6* as _____ is to _____.

    a. 6 : 2   *c.* 12 : 36
    b. 3 : 1   *d.* 12 : 60

Relationship Sentence:

Section 6 Sample Problem

In this problem it is easy to make the error of picking an answer which reverses the relationship between the words. State the relationship between the first pair of words. Then read each of the answer choices aloud and explain whether or not it fits the same relationship. Don't skip any of the answer choices. Read and discuss all four of them.

city is to *mayor* as _____ is to _____.

    a. president : country   *c.* senate : congress
    b. government : business   *d.* business : manager

Relationship Sentence:

Section 7 Sample Problem

This is a difficult question which requires subtle reasoning. Use the same procedure you did with the previous problems. State the relationship between the first pair of words. Then explain fully why each of the answers is either correct or incorrect.

pack is to *wolves* as _____ is to _____.

   a. wheel : spokes   c. alphabet : letters
   b. garage : cars   d. aquarium : fish

Relationship Sentence:

Section 8 Sample Problem

The following problem has a slightly different format, although the idea is the same. The task is to pick the pair of words that form the best analogy when placed in the blanks.

Please do all your reading and thinking aloud. Substitute the first pair of words into the blanks, state any relationship which you see, and explain why the answer does or doesn't form a good analogy. Do this for all four answer choices. Don't skip any of them.

_____ is to *dollar* as *year* is to _____.

a. money : calendar	*c.* penny : century
b. dime : month	*d.* savings : century

Relationship Sentence:

Section 9 Problem Solution

Original Problem

_____ is to *dollar* as *year* is to _____.

    a. money : calendar   *c.* penny : century
    b. dime : month   *d.* savings : century

Problem Solution

_____ is to *dollar* as *year* is to _____.

Money : calendar. Money is to dollar as year is to calendar. A dollar is an amount of money. But a calendar isn't an amount of year. So this doesn't seem like a good analogy.

Dime : month. Dime is to dollar—a dime is one-tenth of a dollar—as year is to month. A year is not part of a month.

Penny : century. Penny is to dollar—a penny is 1/100 of a dollar—as year is to century. A year is 1/100 of a century. So this is a good analogy.

Savings : century. Savings is to dollar as year is to century. A year is part of a century, but savings aren't generally part of a dollar. This doesn't seem to form an analogy.

    The best answer is *c*, penny : century.

Relationship Sentence: A _____ is 1/100 of a _____.

Section 10 Sample Problem

Here is another problem with the new format. Read each of the answer alternatives aloud, substitute the words into the blanks, and explain any relationships that you see. Do this for all four of the answer choices, just as the problem solver did in the last problem solution.

_____ is to *liquid* as *ice* is to _____.

      a. flowing : solid   *c.* water : solid
      b. warm : cold   *d.* milk : cream

Relationship Sentence:

Section 11 Sample Problem

Here is still one more format used with analogy problems. Again, the task is to select the answer which forms the best analogy.

Read each of the answer choices aloud, substitute the words into the blanks, state any relationships you see, and explain why an analogy is or is not formed.

tar is to _____ as *coal* is to _____.

      a. roofing : shovel   *c.* construction : heating
      b. derived : heating   *d.* black : heating

Relationship Sentence:

Section 12 Problem Solution

Original Problem

tar is to _____ as *coal* is to _____.

      a. roofing : shovel   *c.* construction : heating
      b. derived : heating   *d.* black : heating

Problem Solution

Tar is to _____ as *coal* is to _____.

Roofing : shovel. Tar is to roofing as coal is to shovel. Tar is used in roofing, but it doesn't make any sense to say coal is used in shovel.

Derived : heating. Tar is to derived as coal is to heating. Coal is used in heating, but it doesn't make sense to say tar is used in derived.

Construction : heating. Tar is used in construction and coal is used in heating. So this forms an analogy.

Black : heating. Tar is black, but you don't say coal is heating.

    The best answer is *c*, construction : heating.

Relationship Sentence: _____ is used for _____.

Section 13 Sample Problem

Tests sometimes have analogy problems with several answers that form good analogies, but one answer that forms the best analogy. In solving such a problem, try to formulate a relationship sentence which excludes all but one answer, and explains why that answer is best. A good relationship sentence takes the haziness out of deciding which of several good answers is the best one.

Pick the best answer for this problem.

fur is to *bear* as _____ is to _____.

      a. coat : man   *c.* rug : floor
      b. warmth : animal   *d.* wool : sheep

Relationship Sentence:

Why are the following relationship sentences unsatisfactory?

    (A) _____ keeps a _____ warm.

    (A) _____ is a protective covering of a _____.

Section 14 Sample Problem

Pick the best answer for this problem. Use a dictionary if necessary.

centaur is to *horse* as _____ is to _____.

a. woman : mermaid   c. mermaid : fish
b. mermaid : woman   d. fish : mermaid

Relationship Sentence:

Discussion Question

Why is this relationship sentence unsatisfactory?

A _____ is part _____.

Section 15 Sample Problem

Some of the problems in this chapter are quite difficult. Finding the correct answer and the relationship common to the pairs will require an appreciable amount of search and analysis. A good way to work is as follows:

1. Begin with the first answer choice. Try putting the words into the blanks. See if you can find any relationship for the first word pairs. Also, see if you can find any relationship for the second word pairs. If both relationships are clear but not the same, then that answer is not correct. However, if the relationships are not clear, keep this in mind—and perhaps come back to the answer choice later.

2. Do this for each of the answer choices, narrowing down the possibilities.

3. Keep searching until you find an answer which gives you the same relationship for the first half and the second half of the analogy. Do not settle for an answer which is only partially correct. Keep digging until you find one which is totally correct.

4. Carry out your search by asking yourself how the words in each half of the analogy are the same, how they are different, and how they are related.

Here is a difficult problem. If you cannot find the best answer, go back over the steps listed above to be sure you have carried them all out.

_____ is to *cave* as *car* is to _____.

     a. stone : steel   *c.* apartment house : horse
     b. primitive : modern   *d.* modern : primitive

Relationship Sentence:

Section 16 Problem Solution

Original Problem

_____ is to *cave* as *car* is to _____.

      a. stone : steel   *c.* apartment house : horse
      b. primitive : modern   *d.* modern : primitive

Problem Solution

_____ is to *cave* as *car* is to _____.

Stone : steel. Stone is to cave as car is to steel. Stone is what a cave is made of. But car is not what steel is made of. The words would have to be reversed to form an analogy.

Primitive : modern. Primitive is to cave as car is to modern. Primitive is what a cave is. But car isn't what a modern is. The words would have to be reversed to form an analogy.

Apartment house : horse. Apartment house is to cave as car is to horse. The relationships aren't immediately evident here. Perhaps this one should be looked at again later.

Modern : primitive. Modern is to cave as car is to primitive. This answer also seems wrong because the words are reversed. The word *modern* comes before the word *cave*. But the word *primitive* comes after the word *car*.

Answers *a, b,* and *d* seem to be definitely wrong. Answer *c* must be looked at more closely.

Apartment house is to cave as car is to horse. What is the relationship between an apartment house and a cave? There is no obvious relationship.

What is the relationship between a car and a horse? A car is a means of transportation. A horse can also be used for transportation.

How about the relationship between an apartment house and a cave? An apartment house is a place to live. Can a cave be lived in? Yes, cavemen lived in caves, and some animals live in caves. So an apartment house and a cave are similar in that they are both things that can be lived in.

How is an apartment house different from a cave? An apartment house is a modern residence, whereas a cave is primitive.

Now the question is, can this be tied in with the relationship between a car and a horse?

A car and a horse can both be used for transportation. However, a car is a modern means of transportation, while a horse is a more primitive means of transportation.

Therefore, there is a common relationship between the pairs of words. You might say: An apartment house is the modern counterpart of a cave, and a car is the modern counterpart of a horse.

ANALOGY PROBLEMS

For the remaining problems in this chapter your instructor may ask you to work in pairs, taking turns as problem solver and listener. Please remember to read each answer alternative aloud and explain to your partner why you regard it as correct or incorrect. Don't dismiss any answer alternative as incorrect without offering some explanation to your partner. If you do, the communication process with your partner breaks down.

There are a total of 24 problems. After you have worked the first 12 problems, the class will stop and discuss the answers and relationship sentences. Make sure that you have a good reason for each answer, so that you can defend it as correct during the class discussion.

1. *horse* is to *hoof* as _____ is to _____.

     a. man : name   *c.* man : head
     b. man : foot   *d.* animal : run

Relationship Sentence:

2. _____ is to *tennis* as _____ is to *hockey*.

     a. racket : puck   *c.* racket : stick
     b. net : ice   *d.* player : participant

Relationship Sentence:

3. _____ is to *plantation* as *car* is to _____.

     a. Kentucky : Detroit   *c.* agriculture : industry
     b. tractor : passenger   *d.* tobacco : factory

Relationship Sentence:

4. _____ is to *time* as *foot* is to _____.

       a. late : long   *c.* minute : distance
       b. clock : shoe   *d.* space : leg

Relationship Sentence:

5. _____ is to *June* as *July* is to _____.

       a. January : February   *c.* warm : hot
       b. March : September   *d.* March : October

Relationship Sentence:

6. _____ is to *year* as *letters* is to _____.

       a. months : mailbox   *c.* months : alphabet
       b. months : number   *d.* 1974 : A B C

Relationship Sentence:

7. *erosion* is to *soil* as _____ is to _____.

       a. farmland : desert   *c.* polluted : water
       b. exhaustion : work   *d.* demoralization : character

Relationship Sentence:

8. _____ is to *cow* as *mutton* is to _____.

    a. bull : sheep   *c.* beef : pork

    b. calf : sheep   *d.* beef : sheep

Relationship Sentence:

9. _____ is to *torso* as *branch* is to _____.

    a. arm : leaf   *c.* fingernails : acorns

    b. leg : twigs   *d.* arm : trunk

Relationship Sentence:

10. _____ is to *hour* as *hour* is to _____.

    a. minute : second   *c.* clock : minute

    b. minute : day   *d.* minute : long

Relationship Sentence:

11. _____ is to *whiskey* as *refinery* is to _____.

    a. distillery : gasoline   *c.* bottle : barrel

    b. distillery : clothing   *d.* Tennessee : Texas

Relationship Sentence:

12. _____ is to *operation* as *writer* is to _____.

    a. plan : outline   *c.* surgeon : book

    b. hospital : library   *d.* medicine : grammar

Relationship Sentence:

13. _____ is to *time* as *ruler* is to _____.

      a. minute : inch   *c.* clock : length
      b. clock : inch   *d.* clock : straight

Relationship Sentence:

14. _____ is to *exercise* as *salary* is to _____.

      a. running : money   *c.* handball : work
      b. fitness : money   *d.* fitness : work

Relationship Sentence:

15. _____ is to *carbohydrate* as *butcher* is to _____.

      a. baker : meat   *c.* calories : protein
      b. baker : protein   *d.* potato : protein

Relationship Sentence:

16. *hospital* is to *disease* as _____ is to _____.

      a. lawyer : client   *c.* police department : crime
      b. license bureau : license   *d.* United Nations : peace

Relationship Sentence:

17. _____ is to *right* as *weather* is to _____.

      a. wrong : climate   *c.* write : whether
      b. left : rain   *d.* correct : report

Relationship Sentence:

18. *dress* is to *wool* as _____ is to _____.

      a. animal : dog   *c.* door : glass
      b. suit : jacket   *d.* concrete : building

Relationship Sentence:

19. *suit* is to *jacket* as _____ is to _____.

      a. animal : head   *c.* animal : cat
      b. dress : gown   *d.* car : Buick

Relationship Sentence:

20. _____ is to *grass* as _____ is to *sales*

      a. homeowner : customer   *c.* seed : recession
      b. fertilizer : advertising   *c.* weed killer : recession

Relationship Sentence:

21. *whale* is to *dolphin* as _____ is to _____.

      a. gorilla : chimpanzee   *c.* smart : dumb
      b. fish : mammal   *d.* lungs : gills

Relationship Sentence:

22. _____ is to *action* as *seed* is to _____.

      a. idea : flower   *c.* carryout : grow
      b. idea : performance   *d.* act : flower

Relationship Sentence:

23. _____ is to *ocean* as *lake* is to _____.

      a. ship : boat   *c.* Atlantic : Erie
      b. island : land   *d.* rough : calm

Relationship Sentence:

24. *Miami* is to *city* as _____ is to _____.

      a. state : Florida   *c.* city : state
      b. Lincoln : president   *d.* city : south

Relationship Sentence:

Homework Assignment

Make up several analogy problems of the type dealt with in this chapter. For each of them write a problem solution which shows why three answers are incorrect and one is correct.

IX. ANALYSIS OF TRENDS AND PATTERNS

Section 1 Introduction

Patterns and trends are found very frequently in the physical and social sciences, as well as in mathematics. When they occur it is often useful to identify them precisely because they pave the way for predictions about future events. For example, here is the pattern of average minimum temperatures for certain months in New York City.

Year	1973				1974				1975			
Month	Jan.	Apr.	July	Oct.	Jan.	Apr.	July	Oct.	Jan.	Apr.	July	Oct.
Temp. Fahr.	30	47	66	49	29	44	68	46	32	40	68	53

Based on this pattern, approximately what would you expect the average minimum temperatures to be for January, April, July, and October of 1976?

Patterns and trends are found in almost all areas where regular, periodic observation is made. This includes changes in the distances between heavenly bodies; sales records of products ranging from shoes to automobiles; rainfall, wind velocity and other meteorological measures; and even human statistics such as birth, suicide and health patterns. Generally the cycles are more complex and erratic than the simple example above. Nevertheless, by systematically analyzing groups of observations, consistencies are often found which help bring organization to large bodies of facts, and furnish more comprehensible, usable pictures of the universe in which we live.

The problems in this chapter give you practice in identifying patterns and trends among numbers and letters. Not only will your grasp of patterns increase, but because patterns are really recurring relationships, working the problems will also improve your overall skill in analyzing relationships. Furthermore, many students have reported that by going through the problems in this chapter they developed greater confidence and skill in performing arithmetic operations.

Section 2 Sample Problem

This series of letters follows a certain pattern. Try to discover the pattern and write the 3 letters which should come next.

If you are using this book in a class, one student should solve the problem aloud at the chalkboard.

$$A \ B \ A \ C \ A \ D \ A \ E \ \_\_ \ \_\_ \ \_\_$$

There is one more part to this problem. Describe in your own words the pattern of the letters. You may find this a little difficult at first. However, if you were able to decide which 3 letters came next, then you have discovered the pattern.

Write the pattern description below (or on the chalkboard).

Pattern description:

Section 3 Problem Solution

Original Problem

$$A \ B \ A \ C \ A \ D \ A \ E \ \underline{} \ \underline{} \ \underline{}$$

Problem Solution

Problem Solver reads the series, pointing at the letters with her pen, and thinking aloud.	*A B* . . . *A C* . . . *A D*. The series is repeating *A*'s with letters in between that are in alphabetical order. The next one is *E* which is also this pattern. So *A F* and *A G* should follow.
Problem Solver filled the three spaces.	*A B A C A D A E A F A*
Problem Solver wrote the pattern description.	Pattern description: The letter *A* alternates with letters going up the alphabet.

Section 4 Sample Problem

In this problem, numbers are arranged according to a pattern. Identify the pattern, decide which three numbers should come next, and write the pattern description. In a class one student should work the problem aloud at the chalkboard.

3 4 6 7 9 *10* *12* *13* *15* *16* ___ ___ ___

Pattern description:

Section 5 Problem Solution

Original Problem

3 4 6 7 9 10 12 13 15 16 __ __ __

Problem Solution

Problem Solver read and thought aloud, pointing to the numbers with his pen as he read them.	3 4 6 7 9 10 ... 12 13. 3 to 4 is up 1. 6 to 7 is up 1. 9 to 10 is up 1. 4 to 6 is up 2. 7 to 9 is up 2. 10 to 12 is up 2.
Problem Solver wrote these differences above the problem as he computed them.	+ 1 + 2 + 1 + 2 + 1 + 2 3 4 6 7 9 10 12 13 15 16 __ __ __
	It looks like the series goes up 1, up 2, up 1, up 2. Let me check the rest.
	12 to 13—up 1. 13 to 15—up 2. 15 to 16—up 1.
Problem Solver filled the blanks as he computed each answer.	I'll fill in the blanks. The last one was 15 to 16 which was up 1. So next should be up 2 above 16. That would be 18. Then up 1 would be 19. Then up 2 would be 21.
	+ 1 + 2 + 1 + 2 + 1 + 2 + 1 + 2 + 1 + 2 3 4 6 7 9 10 12 13 15 16 18 19 21
Problem Solver wrote the pattern description.	Pattern description: The pattern is add 1, add 2, add 1, add 2, etc.

Section 6 Sample Problem

Decide which 3 numbers should come next in this series and write the pattern description. In a class, one student should work the problem aloud at the chalkboard.

2   7   4   9   6   11   8   13 ___ ___ ___

Pattern description:

Section 7 Problem Solution

Original Problem

2 7 4 9 6 11 8 13 __ __ __

Problem Solution

The Problem Solver read and thought aloud, pointing to the numbers with his pen.	*2 7 4 9 6.* The numbers seem to be going up and down. Let's see the rest. *11 8 13.* Yes, they're going up and down. I'll look at the differences between the numbers to see if there is a pattern. *2* to *7* is up 5. *7* to *4* is down 3. *4* to *9* is up 5. *9* to *6* is down 3. *6* to *11* is up 5.
The Problem Solver wrote each of these differences as he computed it.	+ 5 − 3 + 5 − 3 + 5 2 7 4 9 6 11 8 13 __ __ It seems to be going up 5, down 3, up 5, down 3. I'll check the rest. *11* to *8* is down 3. *8* to *13* is up 5. I'll fill in the blanks. The last pair of numbers were *8* to *13*, which is up 5. So the next should go down 3. *13* minus 3 is *10*. I'll write that in the first blank. + 5 − 3 + 5 − 3 + 5 − 3 + 5 2 7 4 9 6 11 8 13 10 __ __ Next the numbers should go up 5. *10* plus *5* is *15*. I'll write that. + 5 − 3 + 5 − 3 + 5 − 3 + 5 − 3 + 5 2 7 4 9 6 11 8 13 10 15 __ Then they should go down 3. *15* minus 3 is *12*. + 5 − 3 + 5 − 3 + 5 − 3 + 5 − 3 + 5 − 3 2 7 4 9 6 11 8 13 10 15 12 Pattern description: The pattern is add 5, subtract 3, add 5, subtract 3, etc.

Section 8 Writing The Pattern Description

In the last section the problem solver wrote this pattern description:

Pattern description: *Add 5, subtract 3, add 5, subtract 3, etc.*

There are various other ways to phrase this same idea. For example, here is a second way.

Pattern description: *Alternately add 5 and subtract 3.*

Any phraseology which fully expresses this notion is equally good. All that's important is that the pattern description show the basic principle underlying the pattern.

Sometimes different problem solvers will analyze the same pattern in different ways. Here is another way to approach the problem. Notice the numbers that are underlined.

$$\underline{2} \quad 7 \quad \underline{4} \quad 9 \quad \underline{6} \quad 11 \quad \underline{8} \quad 13 \quad \underline{\quad} \quad \underline{\quad} \quad \underline{\quad}$$

These numbers form the series: *2 4 6 8*. This is a series which simply increases by two each time.

Now look at the remaining numbers.

$$2 \quad \underline{7} \quad 4 \quad \underline{9} \quad 6 \quad \underline{11} \quad 8 \quad \underline{13} \quad \underline{\quad} \quad \underline{\quad} \quad \underline{\quad}$$

These numbers form the series: *7 9 11 13*. This series also increases by two each time.

A person could look at the original problem as two separate, alternating series—one starting with 2, the other starting with 7—and both increasing by two. From this point of view a good pattern description would be:

Pattern description: *Two alternating series of numbers, each increasing by two.*

If in working the problems in this chapter, you and your partner come up with different pattern descriptions, first check that they are both really correct. If they are, you will see that they are actually two ways of looking at the same pattern, and both ways will lead to the same answers in filling the blanks.

For some of the problems which you will work later in the chapter, phrasing an accurate pattern description will greatly challenge your verbalizing skills—exercising and strengthening them. The talent to paint in words things that are seen and felt is the distinction of successful writers and public speakers. Teachers are also greatly dependent on this skill if they are to be effective. For example, an excellent gymnastics teacher is able to articulate clearly the positions, the movements, the twists and turns through which a student must direct his body. You have seen in earlier chapters how important vocalizing is in teaching verbal and mathematical problem solving. Teaching in any area means communicating. In fact, for the rest of your life, in both professional and social settings, you will often need to explain things to people. The better you do it, the greater your chances are for vocational advancement and personal happiness.

The Boyer Commission of the Carnegie Foundation states in its report *Reinventing Undergraduate Education* (1998):

> Every university graduate should understand that no idea is fully formed until it can be communicated, and that the organization required for writing and speaking is part of the thought process that enables one to understand material fully. . . . Skills of analysis, clear explanation of complicated materials, brevity, and lucidity should be the hallmarks of communication . . . (p. 24)

For the problems in this chapter, if you can fill the blanks then you know what the pattern is. If the pattern is somewhat complex, don't expect to be able to describe it in just five or ten words. It may take 25 or 30 words—maybe 3 sentences—to describe the pattern fully enough so that someone else can understand it from your description. Take all the time and space necessary to do the job of describing the pattern well.

Section 9 Sample Problem

Write the next 3 entries in this series and the pattern description. In a class, one student should work this problem aloud at the chalkboard.

$$1 \quad z \quad 3 \quad w \quad 9 \quad t \quad 27 \quad q \quad 81 \quad \underline{\quad} \quad \underline{\quad} \quad \underline{\quad}$$

Pattern description:

Section 10 Problem Solution

In reading this problem analysis take special note of three points which may help you in your own problem solving:

1. *One hypothesis considered, checked, rejected, and another one formulated.* At first, the problem solver thought the letters and numbers were related. But after pursuing this for a while and not finding any relationship, she decided to deal with the letters and the numbers separately.

2. *Confusion, error, checking, writing the alphabet, and correction.* In analyzing the letter pattern, the problem solver got confused and made an error. However, good problem solvers continually re-check work that they are in any way unsure about. In re-checking, the problem solver wrote out the alphabet rather than trying to analyze the pattern completely in her own mind. She knew this would lead to greater accuracy, and it allowed her to find and correct her mistake.

3. *Blanks for letters filled first.* The problem solver filled the blanks with the appropriate letters before starting to analyze the numbers. She didn't depend on her memory to recall the letters later. Instead, she wrote them as soon as she figured them out.

Original Problem

1 z 3 w 9 t 27 q 81   ___ ___ ___

Problem Solution

Problem Solver read and thought aloud.	*1 z 3 w 9 t 27 q 81.* The problem has numbers alternating with letters. Let me see if the numbers correspond to the letters in some way. *1 z. Z* is the last letter of the alphabet and 1 is the first number. Maybe the numbers are in reverse order of the letters. *3 w.* Let's see. *s t u v w x y z. W* is not the third letter from the end of the alphabet. The final entries are *q 81.* There aren't 81 letters in the alphabet, so I don't see any relationship between the numbers and the letters. Let me look at just the letters.
	z w t q. These seem to be going backwards in the alphabet. I'll count the letters off. *q r s t.* That's 4 letters. *u v w*—that's 3. *w x y z*—that's 4 again.

*Problem Solver
counted on her
fingers and
wrote the
answers above
the problem.*

$$\overset{4\quad\ 3\quad\ 4}{1\ \ z\ \ 3\ \ w\ \ 9\ \ t\ \ 27\ \ q\ \ 81\ \ \rule{1em}{0.4pt}\ \ \rule{1em}{0.4pt}\ \ \rule{1em}{0.4pt}}$$

Let me check this. I better write out part of the alphabet.

l m n o p q r s t u v w x y z

q . . . r s . . . t. So there are 2 letters in between *q* and *t.*
t . . . u v . . . w. There are 2 letters in between *t* and *w.*
w x y z. There are 2 letters between *w* and *z.* I'll correct
what I wrote.

$$\overset{2\quad\ 2\quad\ 2}{1\ \ z\ \ 3\ \ w\ \ 9\ \ t\ \ 27\ \ q\ \ 81\ \ \rule{1em}{0.4pt}\ \ \rule{1em}{0.4pt}\ \ \rule{1em}{0.4pt}}$$

I wonder what I did wrong before. I guess I was saying that
in going from *q* to *t*, or from *w* to *z*, there are 4 letters if
you include where you start and where you end. But I
made a mistake in going from *t* to *w*. I forgot to count the
first letter, so I only got 3. Anyway, I'll leave it with the
2's. It means that there are 2 letters in between each letter
in the series.

The numbers and letters alternate. Let me fill in the letters
first. The last entry is a number, so the first blank has to
be a letter, then the next one is a number, and the last
one is a letter. So I need 2 letters. I'll look at the part of
the alphabet that I wrote before. From *q*, if I skip back 2
letters I'll be at *n*. I'll write that in the first blank.

$$\overset{2\quad\ 2\quad\ 2}{1\ \ z\ \ 3\ \ w\ \ 9\ \ t\ \ 27\ \ q\ \ 81\ \ n\ \ \rule{1em}{0.4pt}\ \ \rule{1em}{0.4pt}}$$

Now I have to skip over 2 more letters. I'll have to write
out more of the alphabet.

g h i j k l m n o p q r s t u v w x y z

So *k* is the letter for the last blank.

$$\overset{2\quad\ 2\quad\ 2}{1\ \ z\ \ 3\ \ w\ \ 9\ \ t\ \ 27\ \ q\ \ 81\ \ n\ \ \rule{1em}{0.4pt}\ \ k}$$

Now I'll look at the numbers. *1 3 9 27*. It seems to be repeating patterns of 3. No, it's not repeating patterns of 3; instead, *3, 9,* and *27* are all multiples of 3. Let me see. *3* to *9*. Well, 9 is 3 times 3. *9* to *27*. 27 is 3 times 9. *1* to *3*. 3 is 3 times 1. *27* to *81*. I think 3 times 27 is 81. I'll check. 3 times 7 is 21; and 3 times 2 is 6; carry the 2, is 8. So 3 times 27 is 81. It looks like each number is 3 times the previous number.

To fill the blank I need 3 times 81.

$$
\begin{array}{r}
81 \\
\times\ 3 \\
\hline
3 \\
240 \\
\hline
243
\end{array}
$$

```
    2     2     2
1  z  3  w  9  t  27  q  81  n  243  k
```

Pattern description: There are two alternating, independent series, one made up of numbers and the other of letters. Each number is 3 times the previous one. The letters are going backwards, each time skipping 2 letters.

Section 11 Sample Problem

This problem is a little different than the others. However, there is a systematic trend which you can discover through careful analysis, and then use to fill the blanks.

JKLMNO   JKLMON   JKLOMN   JKOLMN _____ _____

Pattern description:

Section 12 Problem Solution

In reading this solution, notice how the problem solver came to identify the trend in small, gradual steps. During her initial reading of the problem, she compared the entries, but only noticed that something was changing near the end of each entry. She didn't even realize that each element involved exactly the same letters. Then she carefully compared the entries again, focusing on the sections that seemed to be changing, and she obtained new information about the types of changes that were occurring. In this way—by making many comparisons and carefully noting the differences from one entry to the next—she was able to pinpoint the trend.

It is generally necessary to make numerous comparisons because your mind can absorb only a limited amount of information at one time. You make comparisons and learn something about the problem. This helps you decide which comparisons to make next. You make more comparisons and you learn more about the problem. Gradually, by noting the similarities, the differences and the changes among the entries, you get a picture of all the relationships existing in the problem. The heart of this process is *numerous, careful comparisons*.

Use this same method in working later problems. Continue to make comparisons until you are sure you understand the relationships completely.

Original Problem

JKLMNO   JKLMON   JKLOMN   JKOLMN _____   _____

Problem Solution

Problem Solver read and thought aloud.	*JKLMNO, JKLMON, JKLOMN.* So far the first 3 letters have remained the same but the last 3 are changing. *JKOLMN.* Now only the first 2 have remained the same and the others are changing. Now I have to try to find out how they are changing. Looking at the first and second ones, *MNO* turns into *MON.* Then *MON* changes to *OMN.* Now I see that each time there are the same letters, but they are changing position. In going from the first to second, the *O* switched places with *N.* Then in going from the second to the third, the *O* switched places with the *M.*
	Let me see. The third is *JKLOMN* and the fourth is *JKOLMN.* Now the *O* switched places with the letter on its left. I guess next time it should switch with the *K.*

In order to fill the blank, I'll look at the fourth entry. *J, K, O, L, M, N.* Now I have to switch the *K* and the *O.* That gives me *J, O, K, L, M, N.*

JKLMNO JKLMON JKLOMN JKOLMN JOKLMN _____

To fill the last blank I'll look at the one I just wrote. It starts *J, O.* I guess I have to switch the *O* with the *J.* That will put the *O* in front. But I guess that's OK. That's what I have to do to be consistent with the rest of the pattern.

JKLMNO JKLMON JKLOMN JKOLMN JOKLMN OJKLMN

Pattern description: All of the entries contain the letters *J, K, L, M, N,* and *O.* In each case, the letters *J, K, L, M,* and *N* remain in alphabetical order. However, the letter *O* switches positions with the letter on its left each time. In other words, the letter *O* moves one position to the left each time.

Section 13 Summary

A good problem solver begins one of these problems by reading along in the series, looking for patterns. He identifies similarities and differences among the entries, and makes mental notes of relationships that he sees. For example, he may observe that the series is composed of letters alternating with numbers, that the numbers seem to be increasing, and that the letters appear to be moving backwards in the alphabet.

As the problem solver gains familiarity with the series, he tries to specify precisely the underlying pattern. He attempts to formulate in his mind some rule which explains how the letters or numbers change in going from one to the next. When he thinks he has found the rule, he checks it against the entire series to be sure it is completely correct. If any part of the series doesn't agree with his rule, he changes his rule until it portrays the entire series accurately.

Finally, when the problem solver is sure his rule is correct, he uses it to fill the blanks, and then writes his rule in the space designated "pattern description."

An important point in working these problems is that the final rule that you formulate and use to fill the blanks must be valid for the entire series. It cannot be only approximately correct. Each of the problems in this chapter was devised according to a definite pattern, and your task is to find a rule which fits (or describes) the pattern.

Quite possibly, as the problems become more difficult, there will be some for which you cannot find the pattern. This does not reflect poor reasoning ability on your part. If you systematically analyze a problem—carefully comparing the elements and looking for relationships—and you still cannot find the overall pattern, it simply means that you have not had background experience with the type of pattern used in that problem. However, if you formulate a sloppy rule—one which does not fit the series perfectly—and if you do not realize that your rule is incorrect because you did not check it carefully—then this is a sure sign of poor reasoning ability. The most serious error that you can make in working these problems is to fill the blanks incorrectly because the rule you formulated does not precisely fit the series. This is pure carelessness. It is much better to leave a question unanswered, than to answer it incorrectly and not recognize your error. The heart of good reasoning is being very careful in formulating your rule, and then thoroughly checking it to determine whether it fits the facts perfectly.

The activities of a good problem solver described above are very similar to the steps preceding many scientific breakthroughs. A scientist such as Charles Darwin observes some facts, gets an idea, collects more facts, formulates the idea precisely into an hypothesis, collects still more facts which either support the hypothesis or lead to a new one, and gradually "discovers" a valid, scientific law. The problems in this chapter can be regarded as miniature problems in scientific analysis and discovery.

Quiz Yourself

1. What is the most serious error that you can make in working the problems in this chapter?

2. Describe in your own words the approach used by good problem solvers in working trend problems.

PROBLEMS IN IDENTIFYING PATTERNS

Work in pairs. If there is a certain problem that you cannot solve after several repeated attempts, ask one of the other pairs for a hint. If that also fails ask your instructor for help.

1. *2 7 10 15 18 23 26 31 34 39* ___ ___ ___

Pattern description:

2. *A B A B B A B A B B A B* ___ ___ ___

Pattern description:

3. *9 a 8 c 7 e 6* ___

Pattern description:

4. *9 12 11 14 13 16 15 18* ___ ___ ___

Pattern description:

5. *B A D C F E H G* __ __ __

Pattern description:

6. *Q Q L Q Q Q Q L L L Q Q L Q Q Q Q L L L Q* __ __ __

Pattern description:

7. *27 24 22 19 17 14 12 9* __ __ __

Pattern description:

8. *A Z B Y C X D* __ __ __

Pattern description:

9. *32 27 29 24 26 21 23* __ __ __

Pattern description:

10. *1 12 121 1212 12121* _____ _____

Pattern description:

11. *8 10 13 17 22 28 35* __ __ __

Pattern description:

12. *147 144 137 141 138 131 135 132 125* ___ ___ ___

Pattern description:

13. *A Z C X E V G* __ __ __

Pattern description:

14. *J 1 P 3 M 5 J 8 P 1 M 3 J 5 P 8 M 1 J 3* P 5 M

Pattern description:

15. *A1 B2 D4 Z26 J10 C3 A1 G7 N14 M13 E 5 A 1 B 2 C 3 __16*

Pattern description:

16. *5 10 20 40 80 160 320 640 1280*

Pattern description:

17. *13R   16P   20N   25L   31J   38H   46F*

Pattern description:

-5 -6 -7 -8 -9 -10 -11
18. *120 115 109 102 94 85 75 64*

Pattern description:

19. *A B C B A 1 2 3 2 1 | A B C B A 1 2 3 2 1 A B C B A*

Pattern description:

20. *B M N* <u>M</u> *B 2 13 14 13 2 B* <u>M</u> *N M B 2* <u>13</u> *14 13 2* <u>B</u> <u>M</u> *N M B*

Pattern description:

$\times 3$

21. *2 6 18 54 162* <u>486</u> <u>1458</u>

Pattern description:

22. *A2 3B B4 3A C2 3D D4 3C E2* <u>3E</u> <u>F4</u> <u>3E</u>

Pattern description:

+1   +2   +3   +4

23. *A A B B D D G G K* <u>K</u> <u>P</u> <u>P</u>

Pattern description:

24. *A C E C E G E G I G* <u>I</u> <u>K</u> <u>I</u>
    B D   D F   F H   H

Pattern description:

25. *64 32 16 8 4* 2 1 .5 .25

Pattern description:

26. *1 11 20* __ *1 A* __ *T K A 1* __ *20 11* __ __ *K T K* __

Pattern description:

27. *ACEG GACE EGAC CEGA* ACCG GACE

Pattern description:

28. *XOXOOOO OXOXOOO OOXOXOO* OODXOXO OOOO XOX

Pattern description:

29. *2 4 3 6 5 10 9 18 17* 34 33 66

Pattern description:

30. *49 48 46 43 39 34* <u>28</u> <u>21</u> <u>13</u>

Pattern description:

31. *8 9 7 10 6 11 5 12* <u>4</u> <u>13</u> <u>3</u>

Pattern description:

32. *1 3 6 8 16 18 36* <u>38</u> <u>76</u> <u>78</u>

Pattern description:

33. *5AA 10BB 12CD 17DG 19EK* <u>E D</u> <u>G</u> <u>V</u>

Pattern description:

34. *D G F H K J L O N P S R* <u>I</u> <u>W</u> <u>V</u>

Pattern description:

35. *1 2 6 24 120* ___ *5040* ___

Pattern description:

36. *1 3 4   7 11 18   2 30 32   5 8 13   5 12* ___   *3 18* ___

Pattern description:

37. *15 4 19   5 80 85   11 2 13   6 3* ___   *4* ___ *14* ___ *8 29*

Pattern description:

38. *2 3 5 8 13 21* ___ ___ ___

Pattern description:

39. *1 2 3 6 11 20 37* ___ ___ ___

Pattern description:

40. *5000 6000 5900 6900 6800 7800 7700* ____ ____ ____

Pattern description:

41. *13 18 20 19 24 26 25 30 32* __ __ __

Pattern description:

42. *4 14 21 26 36 43 48 58 65* __ __ __

Pattern description:

43. *7 3 4 8 4 5 10 6 7 14 10 11 22* __ __ __

Pattern description:

44. *d a a e c c f e e* __ __

Pattern description:

45. *c i o d j p e k q* __ __

Pattern description:

46. *d g h e j k f m n* __ __

Pattern description:

47. *u n g t m f s* __ __

Pattern description:

X. DEDUCTIVE AND HYPOTHETICAL THINKING THROUGH DAYS OF THE WEEK

A businessman had to work late and did not arrive home until early morning for several days, but his wife suspected him of being out with a girlfriend. One early morning he came home and found this note:

> The day before yesterday you did not get home until yesterday; yesterday you did not get home until today. If today you do not get home until tomorrow, you will find that I have left yesterday.

The humorous effect of this note comes from the shifts of perspective in time. The last sentence, for example, uses the fact that by tomorrow, today will be yesterday.

The mental activity involved in following descriptions of this sort—comprehending verbal statements of movements along some dimension and reversing movements by thinking backward through a sequence to see where a movement began—is fundamental in solving many types of mathematics problems. The exercises in this chapter strengthen your ability to follow and graphically represent complicated descriptions, and to change perspectives in reversing operations. Try this sample exercise.

> Suppose my birthday is 2 days after Tuesday. What day is my birthday?

The following diagram shows that 1 day after Tuesday is Wednesday; and 2 days after Tuesday is Thursday.

Tuesday	Wednesday	Thursday
	1 day after Tues.	2 days after Tues.

Therefore, my birthday is on Thursday.

Part I

Each of the following problems is accompanied by a diagram. Show on the diagram all the steps you use to arrive at the answer. Although you may be able to solve the easier problems without a diagram, you will find the diagram indispensable for the more difficult problems that come later.

Exercises

1. Suppose Valentine's Day is 3 days after Friday. What day is Valentine's Day?

W	Th	F	Sa	Su	M	Tu	W

2. Suppose Lincoln's birthday is 4 days before Thursday. What day is Lincoln's birthday?

W	Th	F	Sa	Su	M	Tu	W	Th	F	Sa

3. Suppose Christmas is 2 days after Wednesday?
   a. What day is Christmas?

Th	F	Sa	Su	M	Tu	W	Th	F	Sa

   b. Based on your answer to Part a, what day is 4 days before Christmas?

Th	F	Sa	Su	M	Tu	W	Th	F	Sa

Part II

The next problems are trickier because you must work backward from the given information. Try this sample problem before checking the answer below.

Friday is 2 days after Easter. What day is Easter?

Th	F	Sa	Su	M	Tu	W	Th	F	Sa

Here are the steps you could use to solve the problem. First the given information is represented on the diagram.

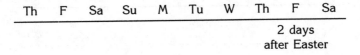

Th	F	Sa	Su	M	Tu	W	Th	F	Sa
							2 days after Easter		

Because Friday is after Easter, we know Easter must be earlier in the week. Thursday is 1 day after Easter.

Th	F	Sa	Su	M	Tu	W	Th	F	Sa
							1 day after Easter		

Therefore, Wednesday must be Easter.

Th	F	Sa	Su	M	Tu	W	Th	F	Sa
						Easter			

Use similar steps in solving the following problems.

Exercises

1. Wednesday is 3 days after Halloween. What day is Halloween?

Th	F	Sa	Su	M	Tu	W	Th	F	Sa

2. Saturday is 5 days before Labor Day. What day is Labor Day?

Th	F	Sa	Su	M	Tu	W	Th	F	Sa

3. The two parts of this exercise contrast the two types of problems you have been solving.
   a. Suppose Christmas is 2 days after Thursday. What day is Christmas?

Th	F	Sa	Su	M	Tu	W	Th	F	Sa

b. Suppose Thursday is 2 days after Christmas. What day is Christmas?

<u>Th   F   Sa   Su   M   Tu   W   Th   F   Sa</u>

Part III

Often in mathematical or other logical problems, you must assume something is true and then deduce conclusions that follow. Here are four ways of presenting information you are asked to assume in deducing a simple conclusion.

Assume today is Tuesday. What is tomorrow?

Suppose today is Tuesday. What is tomorrow?

If today is Tuesday, what is tomorrow?

Today is Tuesday. What is tomorrow?

In reality, today may be Thursday and tomorrow Friday. But each of these four questions asks you to assume today is Tuesday, in which case tomorrow is Wednesday. For the following exercises, assume the given information is true and then deduce the answer requested. Try this problem before checking the answer.

Today is Wednesday. What is 4 days after tomorrow?

<u>W   Th   F   Sa   Su   M   Tu   W   Th   F   Sa</u>

This problem can be easily solved by labeling Wednesday as *today* on a diagram, and then counting off the appropriate days to find the answer.

W	Th	F	S	Su	M	T
↑	↑	↑	↑	↑	↑	
today	tomorrow	1 day after tomorrow	2 days after tomorrow	3 days after tomorrow	4 days after tomorrow	

Exercises

For each exercise, make your own diagram and show the steps you use to reach your answer.

1. Today is Thursday. What is 2 days after tomorrow?

2. Today is Friday. What is 6 days before yesterday?

3. Yesterday was Monday. What is 4 days after tomorrow?

4. Today is Saturday. What is the day after 4 days before tomorrow?

Part IV

Generally, complex mathematical problems are solved by breaking them into parts and working step by step. Consider this problem.

Today is Monday. What is 1 day after 3 days before yesterday?

One way to begin solving such a problem is to separate it into parts like this.

Today is Monday. What is | 1 day after | 3 days before yesterday?

Now we can use a diagram to work step by step through the problem.

Step 1. We are told today is Monday.

Th	F	Sa	Su	M	Tu	W	Th	F	Sa

↑
today

Step 2. This means yesterday was Sunday.

Th	F	Sa	Su	M	Tu	W	Th	F	Sa

↑
yesterday

Step 3. Now we need to find 3 days before yesterday. One day before yesterday was Saturday; 2 days before yesterday was Friday; so 3 days before yesterday was Thursday.

Th	F	Sa	Su	M	Tu	W	Th	F	Sa

↑
3 days
before
yesterday

Step 4. Finally, we need to find 1 day after this.

Th	F	Sa	Su	M	Tu	W	Th	F	Sa

↑
1 day after
3 days
before
yesterday

Note how the four steps correspond to four parts of the original problem.

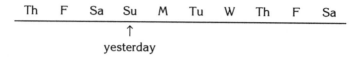

Today is Monday.   What is 1 day after   3 days before   yesterday?

Step 1   Step 4   Step 3   Step 2

Use a similar step-by-step approach in solving the following problems.

Exercises

For each exercise, make your own diagram and show the steps you use to reach your answer. You might find it useful to mark each problem into parts, as shown in the first problem.

1. Today is Friday. What is 2 days before 5 days after yesterday?

2. Today is Thursday. What is 6 days before 3 days after tomorrow?

3. Yesterday was Tuesday. What is 2 days before 4 days after tomorrow?

4. Tomorrow is Sunday. What is 2 days after 3 days before yesterday?

5. Today is Tuesday. What is 2 days after 10 days before the day after tomorrow?

6. Yesterday was Saturday. What is 4 days before 7 days after 2 days before today?

7. You can easily make up new problems by circling alternatives in this problem generator.

				1		1		
	M	1		2		2		yesterday
Today is	W. What is	2 days	before	3 days	before	3	before	today?
	F	3	after	4	after	4	after	tomorrow
				5		5		

Here is an example:

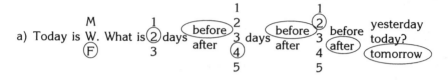

a) Today is W. What is ... yesterday today? tomorrow

b) Generate a problem by circling different alternatives. Then solve the problem, showing all your steps on a diagram.

8. More complicated problems can be created by adding more moves. See if you can analyze this one by separating the moves and working through them one after another. Use a diagram.

Today is Monday. What is 3 days after 2 days before 6 days after 5 days after tomorrow?

Part V

The next set of problems are different from the last set, just as the problems you solved in Part I were different from those in Part II. To see the difference, solve these two problems before checking the answers.

A. Today is Sunday. What is 3 days after today?
B. Sunday is 3 days after today. What is today?

Both problems contain the word *after*. But in Problem A you move to the right to find the answer.

Th	F	Sa	Su	M	Tu	W	Th
			↕			↕	
			today		3 days after today		

For Problem B you move to the left to find the answer because Sunday is already *after* the answer.

Th	F	Sa	Su	M	Tu	W	Th
↕			↕				
today			3 days after today				

Problems like B are generally more difficult because you must reverse your thinking process. When you see the word *after*, you generally do not look for the answer later in the week but earlier—the day mentioned in the assumed information is already *after* the answer. Similarly, when you see *before*, you generally do not look for the answer earlier in the week but later. Try this problem, labeling the diagram fully, before checking the answer.

Sunday is 3 days before yesterday. What was yesterday?

Sa	Su	M	Tu	W	Th	F

Here are the steps you can use to solve the problem.

Step 1. Label the day on the diagram

Sa	Su	M	T	W	Th
	↑				
	3 days before				
	yesterday				

Step 2. Is Sunday before or after yesterday?__before__

Step 3. Which direction is yesterday? __→__

Step 4. Use the diagram to complete the problem.

Sa	Su	M	T	W	Th
	↑	↑	↑	↑	
	3 days before	2 days before	1 day before	yesterday	
	yesterday	yesterday	yesterday		

232   *Deductive and Hypothetical Thinking*

If you have difficulty with any of the following problems, review the simpler but similar problems in Part II. When mathematicians encounter difficulty with a problem, they often examine similar but simpler problems to see how the problems are solved.

Exercises

1. Sunday is 4 days *after* yesterday. What is yesterday?
   a. Label the day on the diagram.

Tu	W	Th	F	Sa	Su	M	Tu

   b. Is Sunday before or after yesterday? _____
   c. Which direction should you move to find yesterday? _____
   d. Find and label yesterday on the diagram.

2. Tuesday is 2 days before tomorrow. What is tomorrow?
   a. Label the day on the diagram.

Sa	Su	M	Tu	W	Th	F	Sa

   b. Is Tuesday before or after tomorrow? _____
   c. Which direction should you move to find tomorrow? _____
   d. Find and label tomorrow on the diagram.

3. Thursday is 3 days after tomorrow. What is today.
   a. Label the day on the diagram.

Su	M	Tu	W	Th	F	Sa	Su

   b. Is Thursday before or after tomorrow? _____
   c. Which direction should you move to find tomorrow? _____
   d. Find and label tomorrow on the diagram.
   e. Find and label today on the diagram.

4. Friday is 3 days before yesterday. What is tomorrow?
   a. Label the day on the diagram.

W	Th	F	Sa	Su	M	T	W

   b. Is Friday before or after yesterday? _____
   c. Which direction should you move to find yesterday? _____
   d. Find and label yesterday on the diagram.
   e. Label today on the diagram.
   f. Label tomorrow on the diagram.

Part VI

The next problems involve two moves. Try this problem before checking the answer.

Monday is 5 days before 2 days after yesterday. What is yesterday?

M	Tu	W	Th	F	Sa

Here are the steps you can use to solve this problem.

Step 1. Separate the problem into two moves

$$\text{Monday is} \ \Big|\ \underset{\text{five days before}}{1}\ \Big|\ \underset{\text{two days after}}{2}\ \Big|\ \text{yesterday.}$$

What is yesterday?

Step 2. Label the day on the diagram.

Su	M	Tu	W	Th	F	Sa

           ↑
    5 days before
      part 2

Step 3. Is Monday 5 days before or after part 2? _before_

Step 4. Which way must you move first? _→_

Step 5. Use the diagram to make the first move. Label the diagram.

Su	M	Tu	W	Th	F	Sa
	↑	↑	↑	↑	↑	↑
	5 days	4 days	3 days	2 days	1 day	Part 2
	before	before	before	before	before	2 days
	Part 2	Part 2	Part 2	Part 2	Part 2	after
						yesterday

Step 6. Which direction must you move in Part 2 to find yesterday? ←

Step 7. Use the diagram to complete the problem. Label your moves.

Su	M	Tu	W	Th	F	Sa
				↑	↑	↑
				yesterday	1 day after	2 days
					yesterday	after
						yesterday

Step 8. Check your answer by starting with Thursday as yesterday and re-versing the steps to see if you reach Monday.

Exercises

1. Monday is 4 days before 1 day after tomorrow. What is tomorrow?
   a. Separate the problem into two moves.
   b. Label the day on the diagram.

F	Sa	Su	M	T	W	Th	F	Sa

   c. Is Monday 4 days before or after Part 2? _____
   d. Which way must you move first? _____
   e. Use the diagram to make the first move. Label the diagram.
   f. Which direction must you move in Part 2 to find tomorrow? _____
   g. Use the diagram to complete the problem.
   h. Check your answer.

2. Thursday is 3 days after the day before yesterday. What is yesterday?
   a. Separate the problem into two moves.
   b. Label the day on the diagram.

Su	M	T	W	th	F	Sa	Su

   c. Is Thursday before or after Part 2? _____
   d. Which way must you move first? _____
   e. Use the diagram to make the first move.
   f. Which direction must you move in Part 2 to find
      yesterday? _____
   g. Use the diagram to complete the problem.
   h. Check your answer

Include a fully labeled diagram that shows all your steps in solving the remaining problems.

3. Wednesday is 6 days before 2 days after tomorrow. What is tomorrow?

4. Monday is 3 days before 2 days before today. What is tomorrow?

5. Sunday is 2 days after 6 days before tomorrow. What is today?

6. Saturday is the day after 3 days after yesterday. What is today?

7. Make up a problem of this type, then solve it showing all your steps on a diagram. Turn it in to your instructor. If you do not have time to complete it in class, do it for homework.

Part VII

The problems you have been solving are complicated counting problems: You count through the days of the week to get the answer. Mathematics has its roots in counting—counting events, objects, and distances—so these are very basic mathematics problems. They require you to think analytically, deductively, graphically, and sometimes in "reverse," the same forms of thinking used in all advanced mathematics.

The exercises in this last section involve both types of problems you have been solving, along with other operations. Use a diagram to solve the "days of the week" portion of each exercise.

Exercises

1. Yesterday was Friday. What is the third letter in the day after tomorrow?

2. If yesterday was Tuesday, is the third letter of 2 days after tomorrow in the first or second half of the alphabet?

3. If 2 days after tomorrow will be Sunday, what position in the alphabet is the first letter of the day before yesterday?

T 20th

4. If 3 days after yesterday is Saturday, how many letters before z in the
   alphabet is the first letter of 4 days before tomorrow?   13

5. If yesterday was Monday, are there more letters in 2 days after tomorrow
   or 3 days after tomorrow?
   Sat. 3days

6. If 6 days ago was Wednesday, what is the second letter after the second
   letter in 2 days after tomorrow?
   d   (Friday)

7. If 6 days after tomorrow is Tuesday, what is the day before 3 days after
   tomorrow?
   Friday

8. If 5 days before the day before tomorrow is Saturday, what is 2 days
   after today?

9. If the day after 3 days after tomorrow is Wednesday, what is 3 days
   before 6 days after yesterday?
   Sunday

10. If the day before 3 days after tomorrow is Wednesday, what is 2 days after 5 days before yesterday?

11. If 4 days $\dfrac{2}{6}$ $\genfrac{}{}{0pt}{}{\text{before}}{\text{after}}$ 5 days $\dfrac{3}{7}$ $\genfrac{}{}{0pt}{}{\text{before}}{\text{after}}$ $\begin{array}{l}\text{yesterday}\\ \text{today}\\ \text{tomorrow}\end{array}$ is $\begin{array}{l}\text{M}\\ \text{T},\\ \text{W}\end{array}$ what is 3 days $\dfrac{2}{4}$

$\genfrac{}{}{0pt}{}{\text{before}}{\text{after}}$ 5 days $\dfrac{3}{7}$ $\genfrac{}{}{0pt}{}{\text{before}}{\text{after}}$ $\begin{array}{l}\text{yesterday}\\ \text{today}\\ \text{tomorrow}\end{array}$?

Select a set of alternatives that generates the *easiest* possible problem for you to solve. Then solve it, showing your steps on a diagram.

12. Select a set of alternatives which generates the *hardest* possible problem for you to solve. Then let your *partner* solve it, showing his work on a diagram.

13. Devise a problem generator like the one in Problem 11, but one that generates harder problems. Use it to generate the hardest problem it can. Then let your partner solve the problem, showing his work on a diagram.

14. Make up a problem like 4. Then let your partner solve it, showing his steps on a diagram.

Extra Practice Problems

1. Wednesday is 5 days before 3 days after tomorrow. What is tomorrow?

2. Tuesday is 4 days before 2 days before today. What is tomorrow?

3. Friday is 2 days after 4 days before tomorrow. What is today?

4. Sunday is the day after 4 days after yesterday. What is today?

5. Friday is the day before 3 days before yesterday. What is tomorrow?

The skills of working step by step and making diagrams that you have learned from this chapter have many applications. In chapter 11, you see how they can be applied to solving mathematical word problems. Step by step reasoning is more important today, in the computer age, than it has ever been. But it has always been the keystone for logic of all kinds. The following three problems are from G. A. Wentworth's 1895 text *Arithmetic*. Approach them in the same manner as you did the earlier problems: work step by step toward your answer and use scratch work or diagrams when helpful.

6. If a workman has taken every day, for the last 12 years, two glasses of beer at 5¢ a glass, how much could he have saved if he had not indulged this habit, reckoning 365 days each year?

7. A man divides $1622.50 among four persons so that the first has $40 more than the second, the second $60 more than the third, and the third $87.50 more than the fourth. How much did the fourth person receive?

8. A man bequeathes to his wife ⅓ of his estate: to his daughter, ⅕ of it; to his son, ½ of the daughter's share: he divides the remainder equally between a hospital and a public library. What part is received by the hospital?

XI. SOLVING MATHEMATICAL WORD PROBLEMS

Section 1 Introduction

People frequently express anxiety and even despair in dealing with mathematical word problems. Generally these feelings stem from unfortunate experiences in early math training. However, just as many people frightened of water have been taught to swim, this chapter has helped many people develop greater confidence and skill in mathematics.

The problems in this chapter are called mathematical word problems. But what does that mean? Simply this: Each problem describes a situation involving numerical relationships. The situation and relationships must first be interpreted and grasped. Then simple arithmetic computations need to be performed to get the answer.

Although these problems are called *mathematical* word problems, they really aren't very different from the nonmathematical problems which you worked earlier. The computations are simple and the use of algebra or formulas is not required. Primarily the problems require that you understand and spell out precisely the situation that is being described. Once a problem has been set up properly, the arithmetic is easy. One of the main things you will learn in this chapter is that if you make a habit of thinking thoroughly and precisely, you can master mathematics. But before turning to the math problems, some general aspects of problem solving will be reviewed.

Section 2 An Expert's Response

As you know, the problem solutions which follow the problems in this book summarize the steps that can be taken in reaching the answers. However, the problem solutions paint a somewhat idealized and perhaps misleading picture. They fail to show the many activities in which good problem solvers become engaged as they analyze a problem and gradually find their way to

241

a solution. Shown on the next page is the actual response of a good problem solver as she solved a problem similar to one you worked earlier. Please read aloud both the comments on the left and the problem solver's response on the right.

Original Problem

If deleting the letters *R*, *I*, and *E* from the word *surmise* leaves a meaningful 3-letter word, circle the first S in this word surmise. Otherwise circle the *U* in the word *surmise* where it appears for the third time in the exercise.

Problem Solver's Response

Problem Solver began reading aloud.	"If deleting the letters *R*, *I*, and *E* from the word *surmise* . . ."
Problem Solver repeated the letters aloud.	"*R, I, E.*"
Problem Solver crossed out the letters R, I, E with her pencil. She then read the remaining letters aloud and pronounced the word they formed.	"*S, U, M, S* . . . Sums.
Problem Solver resumed reading.	"leaves a meaningful 3-letter word, circle . . ."
Problem Solver stopped reading and thought aloud.	I'm getting to the section where I have to do something if the first part is true. I'm a little confused though, maybe I should start reading the sentence from the beginning. No, I'll read the rest of it.
	"circle the first S in this word *surmise*."
	I am confused, let me start again.
	"If deleting the letters *R, I* and *E* from the word *surmise* leaves a meaningful 3-letter word . . ."
	No, sums is a 4-letter word.
	"Circle the first S in this word *surmise*."
	So I won't do this.

"Otherwise circle the *U* in the word *surmise* where it appears for the third time in the exercise.

So this is the direction I'm supposed to follow. Let's see, the word *surmise* appears once . . . twice in the first sentence. Then in the second sentence it appears—3—and that's it. It appears for the third time in the second sentence. So that's the one I should circle. Now I'll reread the last sentence to make sure I followed the directions correctly.

"Otherwise circle the *U* in the word *surmise* where it appears for the third time in the exercise."

I'll scan the sentence again to be sure that the word *surmise* doesn't occur anywhere except the 3 places I found it. Yes, I circled the right one.

Section 3 Another Problem Response

Here is the verbatim response which another problem solver made to a different problem you worked earlier. Again read it aloud, following the problem solver's thoughts and logic.

Original Problem

Sally loaned $7.00 to Betty. But Sally borrowed $15.00 from Estella and $32.00 from Joan. Moreover, Joan owes $3.00 to Estella and $7.00 to Betty. One day the girls got together at Betty's house to straighten out their accounts. Which girl left with $18.00 more than she came with?

Hint: On your diagram, use arrows to show which person has to return money to which other person. Show the direction in which the money must be returned.

Problem Solver's Response

The Problem Solver read aloud.

"Sally loaned $7.00 to Betty. But Sally borrowed $15.00 from Estella and $32.00 from Joan. Moreover, Joan owes $3.00 to Estella and $7.00 to Betty. One day the girls got together at Betty's house to straighten out their accounts. Which girl left with $18.00 more than she came with? Hint: On your diagram, use arrows to show which person has to return money to which other person."

I'll read from the beginning again.

"Sally loaned $7.00 to Betty."
I'll start a diagram with this.

Sally ——————————— $7.00 ——————————— Betty

"But Sally borrowed $15.00 from Estella and $32.00 from Joan." I'll add that to the diagram.

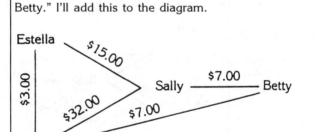

"Moreover, Joan owes $3.00 to Estella and $7.00 to Betty." I'll add this to the diagram.

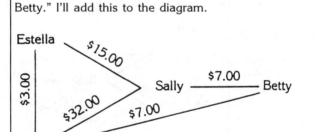

Problem Solver thought aloud.

I have all the numbers in, but I don't know who owes whom what. The hint said something about this. I'll read it again.

"Hint: On your diagram, use arrows to show which person has to return money to which other person."

I guess I have to read back over the problem and put in the arrows as I go.

"Sally loaned $7.00 to Betty."

That means that Betty has to return money to Sally. I'll put an arrow pointing to Sally.

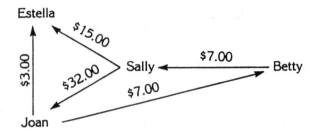

Problem Solver made the additions to the diagram as he read and thought aloud.

"But Sally borrowed $15.00 from Estella . . ."

The money has to be returned to Estella, so I'll draw the arrow pointing to Estella.

"and $32.00 from Joan."

So I'll point the arrow to Joan.

"Moreover, Joan owes $3.00 to Estella . . ."

So I'll point this arrow to Estella.

". . . and $7.00 to Betty."

So this arrow points to Betty.

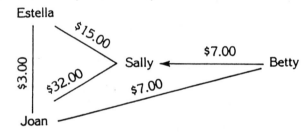

"Which girl left with $18.00 more than she came with?"

Let me figure it out. Looking at my diagram, I see that Joan has to pay $3.00 to Estella and $7.00 to Betty, but she will get $32.00 from Sally. So she has to pay $3.00 plus $7.00 which is $10.00 but she gets $32.00. So she leaves with $22.00.

Betty gets $7.00 from Joan, but pays $7.00 to Sally, so she breaks even.

Estella gets $3.00 from Joan and $15.00 from Sally. She doesn't pay anything out. $3.00 and $15.00 is $18.00. So she's the one who leaves with $18.00.

Let me check Sally to be sure she isn't also $18.00 ahead. She gets $7.00 from Betty. But she pays $15.00 to Estella and $32.00 to Joan. $32.00 and $15.00 is $47.00. She gets $7.00. So she leaves with $40.00 less than when she came.

Section 4 Concern For Accuracy, Step-by-Step Analysis And Subvocal Speech

Two characteristics of good problem solvers were evident in the responses you just read.

First is carefulness: the concern and quick retracking when ideas became confusing; the rechecking, reviewing, and rereading to be sure that errors hadn't crept in, that nothing had been overlooked.

Second is the step-by-step approach. An important example of this was when the problem solvers restated ideas in their own words, in a form which was clearer or more useful to them. For instance, at one place in the last section the problem solver read "Sally loaned $7.00 to Betty." He changed this to "That means Betty has to return money to Sally." This shows that the problem solver went through two steps in representing the information in his diagram. First he translated the original statement to one which was closer to the form he needed for the diagram. Then he incorporated the new statement into his diagram. With the new statement he could more easily see that on the diagram he had to draw the arrow pointing toward Sally. Restating ideas is an important way in which good problem solvers use the step-by-step method to analyze the fine details of a problem.

While on this topic, it should be emphasized that restating ideas—and "talking to themselves" while thinking—is not something good problem solvers do only when they are asked to work a problem aloud. Studies using electronic amplifying equipment (to monitor speech muscle activity) reveal that good problem solvers talk to themselves while they solve problems. They repeat information, rephrase it, weigh it, compare different facts, express thoughts like "I better read the first sentence again," and in general, clarify ideas for themselves. This talking, which is not done aloud, is called covert or subvocal speech.

Quiz Yourself

What is subvocal speech? What do good problem solvers talk to themselves about while solving problems?

Section 5 Sample Ratio Problem

Here is a simple ratio problem. If you are using this book in a class, one student should work the problem aloud.

A train travels 5 mi in 3 min. At this same speed, how far will it travel in 6 min?

This problem tells you the distance that the train travels in 3 minutes—and then asks you to compute the distance it travels in 6 minutes. Six minutes is twice as much time as 3 minutes. If the train travels for twice as much time, it will go twice as far.

This problem is called a *ratio* problem because you first compute the ratio of 6 minutes to 3 minutes. Once you see that 6 minutes is twice as long as 3 minutes, you use that information to calculate the answer.

Ratio problems can become more complicated than this one, and generally there is more than one way to solve them. The ability to solve ratio problems is important in many high school and college courses.

Section 6

Here is another ratio problem. In a class, one student should work it aloud at the chalkboard.

A train can travel 10 mi in 4 min. How far will it travel in 14 min?

Section 7 Several Approaches

Here is the problem you were asked to solve in section 6:

A train can travel 10 mi in 4 min. How far will it travel in 14 min?

There is more than one way to solve this problem. We will look at three ways, which we will call solutions 1, 2, and 3. Each solution can be viewed in terms of the underlying logic, and in terms of the mathematical computations. Looking at the solution in terms of the underlying logic is slower and less elegant. But in a sense it is more important. People who try to apply mathematical formulas without comprehending the underlying logic of a problem stand a good chance of using an incorrect formula and arriving at a wrong answer. Therefore we will begin with the logic and then look at the mathematical computations.

Solution 1

Logic of the Solution: Here is one way to look at the problem. If the train can travel 10 miles in 4 minutes, then it can travel 20 miles in 8 minutes, and 30 miles in 12 minutes. If it travels still another 2 minutes (to make a total of 14 minutes) it will go 5 more miles, for a total of 35 miles. This is shown below:

4 min	10 mi
4 min	10 mi
4 min	10 mi
2 min	5 mi
14 min	35 mi

This is also represented in the following diagram:

10 mi	10 mi	10 mi	5 mi
4 min	4 min	4 min	2 min

Mathematical Solution of the Problem: Notice that in constructing the table above we counted off how many times 4 minutes goes into 14 minutes. We found that it does three times, with 2 minutes left over. At the same time we counted off the same number of 10-mile sections, and concluded that the train travels 35 miles in 14 minutes. We do the same thing arithmetically when we divide 4 minutes into 14 minutes and then multiply this by 10 miles. Thus:

$$14/4 = 3\tfrac{1}{2} \qquad 3\tfrac{1}{2} \times 10 = 35$$

The important thing to understand is that this procedure of dividing and then multiplying is really a shortcut method of spelling out the entire situation, as was done in the table and the diagram above. The diagram shows that we are thinking in terms of 4-minute intervals. In other words, 12 minutes is exactly three 4-minute intervals; and 2 minutes is one-half of a 4-minute interval. Moreover, the train travels 10 miles in each 4-minute interval, and 5 miles in one-half of a 4-minute interval. So it goes 35 miles total.

10 miles	10 miles	10 miles	5 miles
4-minute interval	4-minute interval	4-minute interval	½ of a 4-minute interval

Solution 2

Logic of the Solution: Another way to solve the problem is to think in terms of ratios that are equal to each other. This approach requires more mathematical background and experience than the other two solutions. Don't use this method with any of the later problems in this chapter unless you are absolutely certain you understand exactly what you are doing.

The logic of the solution is shown in the following diagram:

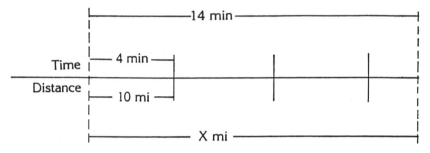

Note the X in the diagram. This is what the problem asks you to find, the distance traveled by the train in 14 minutes.

From the diagram you can see that since 14 minutes is 3½ times more than 4 minutes, the unknown distance X must be 3½ times larger than 10 miles. In other words, the ratio of 14 minutes to 4 minutes is equal to the ratio of X miles to 10 miles. With this idea in mind we can write the following equation:

$$\frac{14}{4} = \frac{X}{10}$$

On the left side of the equation we have the ratio of 14 minutes to 4 minutes. And on the right side we have the ratio of X miles to 10 miles. The equal sign means that these two ratios must be numerically equal.

Mathematical Solution: Once you have set up this equation of ratios, you find X by using simple arithmetic and algebra. Here are steps you could employ:

1. Initial equation: $\dfrac{14}{4} = \dfrac{X}{10}$

2. Multiply both sides of the equation by 10 so that just X will remain on the right side. $\dfrac{10(14)}{4} = \dfrac{X(10)}{10}$

3. Cancel on both sides of the equation. $\dfrac{\overset{(5)\,(7)}{\cancel{10}\cancel{(14)}}}{\underset{1}{\cancel{4}}} = \dfrac{X\,\overset{1}{\cancel{(10)}}}{\underset{1}{\cancel{10}}}$

4. Multiply the numbers to get *X*. $(5)(7) = 35 = X$

Solution 3

Logic of the Solution: A third approach begins by asking how many miles the train travels in 1 minute, and then multiplying this by 14 minutes to find the total distance traveled by the train. The following diagram shows that since the train travels 10 miles in 4 minutes, it must travel 2½ miles in 1 minute.

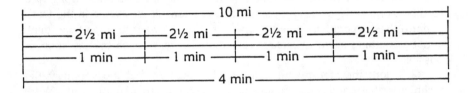

Once we know that the train travels 2½ miles in 1 minute, it is easy to find out how far it travels in 14 minutes. We just add up 14 of these intervals, as shown below.

```
2½ mi   2½ mi   2½ mi   2½ mi   2½ mi
├───────┼───────┼───────┼───────┤ etc. for a total of 14 minutes.
1 min   1 min   1 min   1 min   1 min
```

Mathematical Solution: First you need to determine how many miles the train travels each minute:

$$\frac{10 \text{ mi}}{4 \text{ min}} = 2\frac{1}{2} \text{ mi per min}$$

Once you know that the train travels 2½ miles each minute, you can multiply this by 14 to find how far it travels in 14 minutes.

$$2\frac{1}{2} \text{ mi each min} \times 14 \text{ min} = 35 \text{ mi}$$

Summary

All three solutions are correct. They use different computational approaches and formulas, but they are based on basically the same picture of what happens as the train's traveling time increases from 4 minutes to 14 minutes.

Procedure for Solving Math Word Problems

This section reviews the procedure for solving math word problems while using the thinking aloud pair problem solving technique with a partner.

1. Try to do all your thinking aloud. Read aloud and vocalize (think-aloud) all of your thoughts, decisions, analyses, and conclusions. Vocalize how you are starting the problem, questions you are asking yourself, steps you are taking in breaking the problem into parts, conclusions you are drawing—everything. If you have to add some numbers, add them aloud. If you perform any other mental operations (such as translating an unfamiliar word to a familiar word, or visualizing a picture of a relationship described in the text), perform these operations aloud. If you occasionally want to reread and think about something silently, explain your thoughts to your partner as soon as possible.

2. Adopt the step-by-step analytical procedure and the various other techniques that good problem solvers use. Break a problem into parts. Work one part accurately and then move on to the next part. Translate unfamiliar or unclear phrases into your own words. Visualize or make diagrams of relationships presented verbally. Simplify a problem by substituting easier numbers, making a table of successive computations, or referring to an earlier problem.

3. Be extremely accurate. Continually check your thinking. In the back of your mind there should always be the thought: "Is that entirely correct? . . . Is that completely accurate?" Never work so quickly that it leads to errors. Work everything slowly and carefully. Give sufficient time to all parts of the problem. Never just give up on a problem and guess an answer. Always try to reason the problem out.

4. While another student is working a problem, check his accuracy so that he will learn to think with more precision and thoroughness. In addition, in your own mind contrast his method with the way you might attack the same problem. How might you break the problem down more completely into subproblems? What other steps might you take? How might you visualize or diagram certain relationships? Would you work more carefully and accurately? In other words, try to imagine ways in which you might attack the problem more effectively.

Section 8 Sample Problem

Try this problem. It is in some ways similar, but in other ways different from the last one. In a class, one student should solve the problem aloud at the chalkboard, explaining his logic completely.

> A certain ruler, which is supposed to be 12 in long, is warped and is actually just 11½ in. If you measure off 4 ft of string with this ruler, how long would the string really be?

Section 9 Problem Solution

Original Problem

A certain ruler, which is supposed to be 12 in long, is warped and is actually just 11½ in. If you measure off 4 ft of string with this ruler, how long would the string really be?

Problem Solution

A good way to begin this problem is to imagine yourself actually taking a ruler and measuring off 4 feet of string. You might picture a ball of string on a table and see yourself pulling out the string and laying off 1 foot at a time using the ruler.

The ruler is supposedly 12 inches long, and 12 inches is 1 foot. Each time you measure off a section of string equal to the length of the ruler, you supposedly have 1 foot of string. Since you want 4 feet, you will have to do this four times.

However, the ruler is warped, so each section of string is only 11½ inches long. Therefore when you measure off four sections of string, the total length is:

$$4 \times 11\tfrac{1}{2} \text{ in} = 46 \text{ in}$$

There are several alternate ways of doing this problem. In picturing yourself laying off four sections of string with the ruler, you might calculate how much your accumulated error is.

The ruler is 11½ inches, so each time you lay off a section of string with the ruler you are ½ inch short of the full 12 inches. When you lay off four sections of string with the ruler, you will be four times that short:

$$4 \times \tfrac{1}{2} \text{ in short} = 2 \text{ in short}$$

Since you are 2 inches short of the full 48 inches, your string will actually be 46 inches long.

$$48 \text{ inches} - 2 \text{ inches} = 46 \text{ inches}$$

A third way of approaching this problem is to look at it in terms of ratios. In the diagram below we let X inches be the unknown length of the string measured off with the warped ruler. The diagram shows that there are as many 12-inch sections in 48 inches as there are 11½ inch sections in X inches.

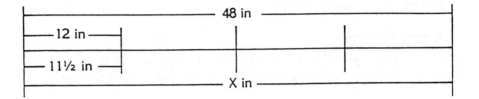

From the diagram we see that because 48 divided by 12 is four, we know that X divided by $11\frac{1}{2}$ must also be four. The ratio of 48 to 12 is equal to the ratio of X to $11\frac{1}{2}$. In mathematical symbols we write that this way:

$$\frac{48}{12} = \frac{X}{11\frac{1}{2}}$$

To solve this equation you could employ the following steps:

1. Initial equation:

$$\frac{48}{12} = \frac{X}{11\frac{1}{2}}$$

2. Multiply both sides of the equation by $11\frac{1}{2}$, to obtain just X on the right side.

$$\frac{(11\frac{1}{2})48}{12} = \frac{X(11\frac{1}{2})}{11\frac{1}{2}}$$

3. Cancel.

$$\frac{(11\frac{1}{2})\overset{4}{\cancel{48}}}{\underset{1}{\cancel{12}}} = \frac{X(\cancel{11\frac{1}{2}})}{\underset{1}{\cancel{11\frac{1}{2}}}}$$

4. Multiply to get X.

$$(11\frac{1}{2})4 = 46 = X$$

Look back at problem 1 on page 232. In what ways is that problem similar to this one? In what ways is it different?

Section 10 Sample Problem

Some of the math word problems in this chapter are quite different from the ratio or rate problems you have just worked. Here is an example. In a class, one student should solve the problem aloud at the chalkboard.

Ted's weekly income is $100.00 less than double Gary's weekly income. If Ted makes $500.00 a week, what does Gary make?

Section 11 Problem Solution

Original Problem

> Ted's weekly income is $100.00 less than double Gary's weekly income. If Ted makes $500.00 a week, what does Gary make?

Problem Solution

Whenever it is possible to represent the ideas of a math problem with a diagram, it is generally useful to do so. We will use a diagram to help keep track of the facts in this problem.

The first sentence says Ted's weekly income is $100.00 less than double Gary's weekly income. We'll draw a line to represent income and then place Ted on it.

$$\vdash \text{Ted's income}$$

Since Ted's income is $100.00 less than double Gary's, it means that on the diagram Ted's income should be below (less) double Gary's income. Therefore we'll place "double Gary's income" above Ted's income, separated by $100.00.

$$
\begin{array}{l}
\vdash \ 2 \times \text{Gary's income} \\
\quad\ \ \uparrow \\
\quad\ \ \$100 \\
\quad\ \ \downarrow \\
\vdash \ \text{Ted's income}
\end{array}
$$

Check the diagram. Does it show what it is supposed to show, namely that Ted makes $100.00 less than double Gary?

Finally, the problem says that Ted makes $500.00. We'll add that to the diagram.

$$
\begin{array}{l}
\qquad\quad \vdash \ 2 \times \text{Gary's income} \\
\qquad\qquad\ \ \uparrow \\
\qquad\qquad\ \ \$100 \\
\qquad\qquad\ \ \downarrow \\
\$500 \ \vdash \ \text{Ted's income}
\end{array}
$$

From the diagram we see that double Gary's income is $100.00 more than Ted's income—which means it is $600.00.

$600 ─┬─ 2 × Gary's income

      │ $100

$500 ─┴─ Ted's income

Since double Gary's income is $600.00, his actual income must be one-half of that:

$$½($600) = $300$$

In working this problem there is a common error made, especially if a diagram is not used to help keep track of the relationships. As soon as beginners see the words "less than" they often automatically conclude that they should subtract. Their reasoning goes something like this: "Ted's income is $100.00 less than double Gary's income. Ted makes $500.00 a week: $100.00 less than that is $400.00. So double Gary's income is $400.00 and ½ of that is $200.00."

Do you see where the error was made in this train of thought? Before continuing, review and explain it in your own words.

This faulty reasoning comes from dealing carelessly or superficially with the words "less than," rather than spelling out exactly which income is less than which. In all of the problems that follow, spell out fully and precisely the relationships among the facts. And whenever you feel a little doubtful or confused, try to use a diagram.

Now look back at problem 3 on page 47. In what ways are the two problems similar? In what ways are they different?

Section 12 Sample Problem

Work this problem by representing the facts of the first sentence in one diagram, and then the second sentence in a separate diagram. In a class, one student should work the problem aloud at the chalkboard.

> Paul makes $25.00 a week less than the sum of what Fred and Carl together make. Carl's weekly income would be triple Steven's if he made $50.00 more a week. Paul makes $285.00 a week and Steven makes $75.00 a week. How much does Fred make?

Section 13 Problem Solution

Original Problem

Paul makes $25.00 a week less than the sum of what Fred and Carl together make. Carl's weekly income would be triple Steven's if he made $50.00 more a week. Paul makes $285.00 a week and Steven makes $75.00 a week. How much does Fred make?

Problem Solution

The first sentence says Paul makes $25.00 a week less than the incomes of Fred and Carl combined. So we'll make a diagram with Paul placed $25.00 below Fred plus Carl.

```
  ┼ Fred + Carl
  │  $25
  ┼ Paul
```

The second sentence says Carl's weekly income would be triple Steven's if he made $50.00 more a week. In other words, if we go up $50.00 from Carl's income it will bring us to triple Steven's income. This is shown in the diagram on the right.

```
  ┼ Fred + Carl                    ┼ 3 × Steven's income
  │  $25                           │  $50
  ┼ Paul                           ┼ Carl
```

The problem says Paul makes $285.00 a week. When we add that to the diagram, we see that Fred plus Carl combined make $310.00.

```
$310 ┼ Fred + Carl                 ┼ 3 × Steven's income
     │  $25                        │  $50
$285 ┼ Paul                        ┼ Carl
```

The problem also says that Steven makes $75.00 a week. Therefore triple Steven's income is: $3 \times \$75 = \$225$. The diagram on the right shows that Carl makes $50.00 less than this, so Carl must make $175.00 a week.

$310 ┼ Fred + Carl $225 ┼ 3 × Steven's income

        $25 $50

$285 ┼ Paul $175 ┼ Carl

We now know that Carl's income is $175.00 a week, and we also know that the sum of Fred's plus Carl's incomes is $310.00 a week. From this we can determine Fred's income by subtraction.

$$\$310 - \$175 = \$135$$

MATH WORD PROBLEMS

Introduction

Your instructor may ask you to work in pairs, taking turns solving the following problems aloud. In working the problems, make sure you understand the underlying logic before you apply any formulas. First take some time to spell out in your mind (or in a table or diagram) what the actual situation is, and only then start to make your mathematical computations. This is the key to working mathematical word problems correctly.

Special Instruction for Listeners

If your partner performs computations or applies formulas that are inappropriate and lead to wrong answers—or has not spelled out situations with full understanding—*insist* that you be shown a table or diagram which illustrates, step-by-step, the relationships between the facts in the problem. Stopping your partner and requesting a full explanation of certain computations is your responsibility in helping both of you become good mathematical problem solvers.

Problem 1

John can run 7 ft in the time that Fred runs 5 ft. How far will John run in the time that Fred runs 15 ft?

Original Problem

John can run 7 ft in the time that Fred runs 5 ft. How far will John run in the time that Fred runs 15 ft?

Problem Solution

Logic of the Solution: If John can run 7 feet when Fred runs 5, then John can run 14 feet when Fred runs 10, and he can run 21 feet when John runs 15. This is shown in the table below.

Fred	John
5	7
5	7
5	7
15	21

Mathematical Solution:

Step 1. When Fred runs 15 feet, how many times further does he run compared to when he runs only 5 feet? To answer this you divide:

$$15/5 = 3.$$

Step 2. If Fred runs three times as far, he must run three times as long.

Step 3. When John also runs three times as long, how much distance does he cover? The answer is $7 \times 3 = 21$ feet.

This diagram shows that every time Fred runs 5 ft, John runs 7 ft.

When Fred runs 15 ft, John runs 21 ft.

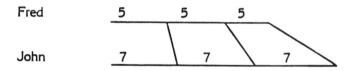

Problem 2

A train travels 30 mi in the time a car travels 20 mi. At that rate, how far will the train travel when the car travels 90 mi?

Original Problem

A train travels 30 mi in the time a car travels 20 mi. At that rate, how far will the train travel when the car travels 90 mi?)

Problem Solution

Logic of the Solution: If the train travels 30 miles when the car travels 20, then the train travels 60 miles when the car travels 40, it travels 90 miles when the car travels 60, it travels 120 miles when the car travels 80, and it travels 135 miles when the car travels 90. This is shown below.

20 mi	20 mi	20 mi	20 mi	10 mi
30 mi	30 mi	30 mi	30 mi	15 mi

Mathematical Solution:

Step 1. We need to know how many times as far the car travels when it goes 90 miles compared to when it goes 20 miles.

$$90/20 = 4\frac{1}{2} \text{ or } 4.5$$

Step 2. If the car travels 4.5 times as far in going 90 miles, it must travel 4.5 times as long. When the train travels 4.5 times as long, it goes this far: 4.5×30 miles.

$$
\begin{array}{r}
30 \\
\times\, 4.5 \\
\hline
15\,0 \\
120 \\
\hline
135.0
\end{array}
$$

The train travels 135 miles when the car travels 90 miles.

Problem 3

Be careful to notice the difference between feet and yards in this problem.

If Fidel runs 4 yds in the time Sadam runs 9 ft, how many ft does Sadam run when Fidel runs 120 ft?

Original Problem

If Fidel runs 4 yds in the time Sadam runs 9 ft, how many ft does Sadam run when Fidel runs 120 ft?

Problem Solution

Step 1. One yard is 3 feet. So 4 yards equals 12 feet.

The problem can be restated like this:

If Fidel runs 12 ft in the time Sadam runs 9 ft, how many ft does Sadam run when Fidel runs 120 ft?

Step 2. We need to know how many times as far Fidel goes when he runs 120 feet compared to when he runs 12 feet.

$$\frac{120}{12} = 10$$

Step 3. If Fidel travels 10 times as far in going 120 feet, he must travel 10 times as long. During that same time Sadam would also run 10 times as far:

$$10 \times 9 \text{ feet} = 90 \text{ feet}$$

Problem 4

A man runs 1 mi in 10 min and a car goes 50 mi an hr. At these rates, how far does the man go when the car goes 150 mi?

Original Problem

A man runs 1 mi in 10 min and a car goes 50 mi an hr. At these rates, how far does the man go when the car goes 150 mi?

Problem Solution

Step 1. One way to work this problem is to determine how much time the car takes to go 150 miles, and then find how far the man runs in the same time.

Step 2. The car goes 150 miles, and it covers 50 miles each hour. Therefore the number of hours it travels is:

$$\frac{150}{50} = 3 \text{ hrs}$$

This means the man also runs for 3 hours.

Step 3. The problem says the man runs 1 mile every 10 minutes. Since an hour has 60 minutes (which is 6 times as long as 10 minutes) he runs 6 miles an hour. Therefore in 3 hours he runs:

$$3 \text{ hrs} \times 6 \text{ mi per hr} = 18 \text{ mi}$$

Problem 5

A car travels 40 mi an hr and a plane travels 10 mi a min. How far will the car travel while the plane travels 450 mi?

Original Problem

> A car travels 40 mi an hr and a plane travels 10 mi a min. How far will the car travel while the plane travels 450 mi?

Problem Solution

Step 1. We can work this problem by determining how much time the plane takes to go 450 miles, and then finding out how far the car goes in the same time.

Step 2. Since the plane goes 450 miles, and it travels 10 miles each minute, it's traveling time is:

$$\frac{450}{10} = 45 \text{ min}$$

Step 3. This means the car also travels for 45 minutes. The problem says it travels 40 miles an hour. Let's figure out how far it travels per minute. Since there are 60 minutes in an hour, the car will travel 1/60 of 40 miles in a minute.

$$\frac{1}{60} (40 \text{ mi}) = \frac{2}{3} \text{ mi}$$

Step 4. The car travels 2/3 of a mile each minute. In 45 minutes it will go:

$$45 \text{ min} \times \frac{2}{3} \text{ mi per min} = 30 \text{ mi}$$

Problem 6

Clock *A* keeps perfect time whereas clock *B* runs fast. When clock *A* says 6 min have passed, clock *B* says 8 min have passed. How many minutes have really passed when clock *B* says 56 min have passed?

Original Problem

> Clock *A* keeps perfect time whereas clock *B* runs fast. When clock *A* says 6 min have passed, clock *B* says 8 min have passed. How many minutes have really passed when clock *B* says 56 min have passed?

Problem Solution

Step 1. The question is how many minutes have passed according to clock *A* (which is accurate) when clock *B* shows that 56 minutes have passed.

Step 2. When clock *B* says 8 minutes have passed, actually only 6 minutes have passed. When clock *B* says 16 minutes have passed, only 12 minutes have passed.

Clock B	Clock A (Accurate)
8	6
8	6
—	—
—	—

Step 3. It is necessary to find out how many 8-minute intervals there are in 56 minutes.

$$\frac{56}{8} = 7$$

Step 4. So the actual time that passed is 7 intervals of 6 minutes each.

$$7 \times 6 \text{ minutes} = 42 \text{ minutes}$$

Step 5. The actual time that passed is 42 minutes.

Clock B	Clock A (Accurate)
8	6
8	6
8	6
8	6
8	6
8	6
8	6
56	42

Problem 7

Clock *A* keeps perfect time whereas clock *B* runs fast. When clock *A* says 4 min have passed, clock *B* says 6 min have passed. How many minutes have really passed when clock *B* says 27 min have passed?

Original Problem

Clock *A* keeps perfect time whereas clock *B* runs fast. When clock *A* says 4 min have passed, clock *B* says 6 min have passed. How many minutes have really passed when clock *B* says 27 min have passed?

Problem Solution

Step 1. The question is how many minutes have passed according to clock *A* (which is accurate) when clock *B* shows that 27 minutes have passed.

Step 2. When clock *B* says 6 minutes have passed, actually only 4 minutes have passed. When clock *B* says 12 minutes have passed, only 8 minutes have passed.

Clock B	Clock A (Accurate)
6	4
6	4
—	—
—	—

Step 3. It is necessary to find out how many 6-minute intervals there are in 27 minutes.

$$\frac{27}{6} = 4\frac{1}{2}$$

Step 4. So the actual time that passed is 4½ intervals of 4 minutes each.

$$4\frac{1}{2} \times 4 \text{ minutes} = 18 \text{ min}$$

Step 5. The actual time that passed is 18 minutes.

Clock B	Clock A (Accurate)
6	4
6	4
6	4
6	4
3	2
27	18

Problem 8

A certain clock runs fast, gaining 6 min every hour. If it is set correctly at 3:00, what time will it show when the correct time is 7:30?

Original Problem

A certain clock runs fast, gaining 6 min every hour. If it is set correctly at 3:00, what time will it show when the correct time is 7:30?

Problem Solution

Step 1. From 3:00 to 7:30 is 4½ hours.

Step 2. The clock gains 6 minutes every hour. In 4 hours it will gain 24 minutes, and in ½ hour it will gain 3 minutes. So in 4½ hours it will gain 27 minutes.

$$4½ \times 6 = 27$$

Step 3. 7:30 plus 27 minutes is 7:57.

The clock will read 7:57.

True Time	Clock Reads
4:00	4:06
5:00	5:12
6:00	6:18
7:00	7:24
7:30	7:57

Problem 9

A certain clock runs fast; it indicates 1 hr has passed when actually only 56 min have passed. If it is set correctly at 1:00, what is the correct time when it reads 6:30?

Original Problem

A certain clock runs fast; it indicates 1 hr has passed when actually only 56 min have passed. If it is set correctly at 1:00, what is the correct time when it reads 6:30?

Problem Solution

Step 1. Every time the clock shows an hour having passed, actually 4 minutes less than an hour has passed. When the clock shows 2 o'clock, it is really 1:56. When it shows 3:00, it is really 2:52.

Clock	Correct Time
1:00	1:00
2:00	1:56
3:00	2:52

Step 2. When the clock moves from 1:00 to 6:30, it moves 5½ hours. For each hour on the clock, the true time that passed is 4 minutes less than an hour. So when the clock says that 5½ hours have passed, the true time that passed is less than that by the amount:

5½ hrs × 4 min less per hour = 22 min less

Step 3. When the clock reads 6:30, the true time is 22 minutes less than this:

6:30 minus 22 min = 6:08

Clock	Error	Correct Time
1:00		1:00
2:00	4 min.	1:56
3:00	8 min.	2:52
4:00	12 min.	3:48
5:00	16 min.	4:44
6:00	20 min.	5:40
6:30	22 min.	6:08

Problem 10

Clock *A* loses 4 min every half hour, and clock *B* gains 5 min every 2 hrs. Both clocks are set correctly at 5:00 P.M. How many minutes apart are they when the true time is 9:00 P.M.?

Original Problem

> Clock *A* loses 4 min every half hour, and clock *B* gains 5 min every 2 hrs. Both clocks are set correctly at 5:00 P.M. How many minutes apart are they when the true time is 9:00 P.M.?

Problem Solution

Step 1. From 5:00 P.M. to 9:00 P.M. is a total period of 4 hours.

Step 2. Clock *A* loses 4 minutes every half hour. That means it loses 8 minutes every hour. So in 4 hours it will be behind by this amount:

$$4 \text{ hrs} \times 8 \text{ min every hour} = 32 \text{ min}$$

Step 3. Clock *B* gains 5 minutes every 2 hours. Therefore in 4 hours it gains 10 minutes.

Step 4. So far we have determined that clock *A* will be 32 minutes behind when the correct time is 9:00 P.M., and clock *B* will be 10 minutes ahead. That means they will be 42 minutes apart.

Problem 11

A 12-in ruler is poorly constructed and is really 12½ in long. You measure off what you believe is 5 yrds of string with this ruler. What is the true length of the string?

Original Problem

A 12-in ruler is poorly constructed and is really 12½ in long. You measure off what you believe is 5 yrds of string with this ruler. What is the true length of the string?

Problem Solution

Step 1. Each time you measure off a section of string equal in length to the ruler, it is really 12½ inches long.

Step 2. You want 5 yards of string. Since there are 3 feet in a yard, this is 15 feet of string.

Step 3. When you measure off 15 sections of string, each equal to the length of the ruler, the total length of string is:

$$15 \times 12\tfrac{1}{2} \text{ in} = 187\tfrac{1}{2} \text{ in}$$

$$
\begin{array}{r}
15 \\
\times\ 12.5 \\
\hline
75 \\
30\ \\
15\ \ \\
\hline
187.5 \\
\end{array}
$$

Problem 12

How many inches short would a piece of cloth be if you measure off 24 ft of cloth with a yardstick that is warped and is 2 in short?

Note: A yardstick is 1 yrd, and 1 yrd equals 3 ft.

Original Problem

How many inches short would a piece of cloth be if you measure off 24 ft of cloth with a yardstick that is warped and is 2 in short?

Note: A yardstick is 1 yrd, and 1 yrd equals 3 ft.

Problem Solution

Step 1. Each time you measure off a yardstick's length of material it is 2 inches short. When you measure off 2 yards it is 4 inches short, when you measure off 3 yards it is 6 inches short.

Measured Length (yrd)	Error (in)
1	2
2	4
3	6

Step 2. It is necessary to determine how many times the yardstick would be used in measuring off 24 feet of material. One yard is 3 feet. Two yards is 6 feet. Three yards is 9 feet. Four yards is 12 feet. Five yards is 15 feet. Six yards is 18 feet. Seven yards is 21 feet. Eight yards is 24 feet.

So the yardstick will be applied eight times, and each time it is in error by 2 inches. Therefore, the total error will be:

$$8 \times 2 \text{ in} = 16 \text{ in}$$

Step 3. Thus, the piece of material would be 16 inches short.

Measured Length (yrd)	Error (in)
1	2
2	4
3	6
4	8
5	10
6	12
7	14
8	16

Problem 13

Boris owns 6 suits, 3 less than Che and twice as many as Phylis. Gene owns 3 times as many suits as Che. How many suits each do Gene and Phylis own?

Note: Knowledge of algebra is not required in solving this problem or the ones that follow. All that is required is that you read the problem carefully, determine what it is asking, determine what information and what relationships are given, and then work through the relationships accurately.

Original Problem

> Boris owns 6 suits, 3 less than Che and twice as many as Phylis.
> Gene owns 3 times as many suits as Che. How many suits each do
> Gene and Phylis own?

Problem Solution

Step 1. Boris owns 6 suits.

Boris—6

Step 2. Boris owns 3 suits less than Che. That means Che owns 3 more suits
than Boris, so Che owns 9 suits.

Boris—6   Che—9

Step 3. Boris owns twice as many suits as Phylis. This means Phylis owns
only half as many suits as Boris. Since Boris owns 6 suits, Phylis
owns 3 suits.

Boris—6   Che—9   Phylis—3

Step 4. Gene owns 3 times as many suits as Che. Che owns 9 suits, so Gene
owns 27 suits.

Boris—6   Che—9   Phylis—3   Gene—27

Step 5. How many suits each do Gene and Phylis own?

Gene owns 27, Phylis owns 3.

Problem 14

The number of cows owned by farmer Smith is the number owned by farmer Thompson divided by the number owned by farmer Jones. If farmer Thompson, who owns 42 cows, had 14 more cows, he would own 8 times as many cows as farmer Jones. How many cows does farmer Smith own?

Original Problem

The number of cows owned by farmer Smith is the number owned by farmer Thompson divided by the number owned by farmer Jones. Farmer Thompson, who owns 42 cows, would own 8 times as many cows as farmer Jones if he owned 14 more cows. How many cows does farmer Smith own?

Problem Solution

Step 1. The problem asks how many cows farmer Smith owns.

Step 2. The number of cows owned by Smith is the number owned by Thompson divided by the number owned by Jones.

$$\text{Smith's cows} = \frac{\text{Thompson's cows}}{\text{Jones cows}}$$

Step 3. Thompson has 42 cows.

$$\text{Thompson—42 cows}$$

Step 4. If Thompson owned 14 more cows he would own eight times as many cows as Jones.

$$\text{Thompson's cows} + 14 = 8 \times \text{Jones' cows}$$

Step 5. If Thompson owned 14 more cows he would own:

$$42 + 14 = 56 \text{ cows}$$

Step 6. So 56 cows is eight times as many cows as Jones owns.

$$56 = 8 \times \text{Jones' cows}$$

Step 7. To find Jones' cows divide 56 by 8.

$$\text{Jones's cows} = \frac{56 \text{ cows}}{8} = 7 \text{ cows}$$

Step 8. To get the number of cows owned by Smith, the division shown in step 2 must be carried out.

$$\text{Smith's cows} = \frac{42}{7} = 6 \text{ cows}$$

Step 9. Smith owns 6 cows.

Problem 15

If Bo's weekly income doubled he would be making $500.00 a week more than Om. Bo's weekly income is $700.00 more than one-half of Phi's. Phi makes $1800.00 a week. How much does Om make?

Original Problem

If Bo's weekly income doubled he would be making $500.00 a week more than Om. Bo's weekly income is $700.00 more than one-half of Phi's. Phi makes $1800.00 a week. How much does Om make?

Problem Solution

Step 1. Strategy for working this problem: The problem asks for Om's income. It gives Phi's income as $1800.00. It also tells how to get from Phi's income to Bo's income, and then from Bo's income to Om's income.

Step 2. It says Phi's income is $1800.00 and it says Bo's income is $700.00 more than one-half of this. So if Phi's income is divided in half, and then $700.00 is added, we will have Bo's income.

$$\frac{\text{Phi's income}}{2} + \$700 = \text{Bo's income}$$

$$\frac{\$1800}{2} + \$700 = \$900 + \$700 = \$1600 = \text{Bo's income}$$

Step 3. Thus, Bo's income is $1600.00 a week.

Step 4. It says that double Bo's income is $500.00 more than Om's. 2 × Bo's income is $500.00 more than Om's income.

Step 5. Double Bo's income is: 2 × $1600 = $3200.

Step 6. So, $3200.00 is $500.00 more than Om's income. Therefore, Om's income is $3200 − $500 = $2700.

Problem 16

Pau owns 4 more than one-half as many books as Ete. Pau owns 32 books. How many books does Ete own?

Note: After you solve the problem, please read the problem solution—even if your answer is correct. The problem solution illustrates a principle which is used in the remaining four problems of the program.

Original Problem

> Pau owns 4 more than one-half as many books as Ete. Pau owns 32 books. How many books does Ete own?

Problem Solution

Step 1. A diagram can be used to clarify the relationship between Pau's books and Ete's books. Starting at Ete's books, we take one-half of them.

┼ Ete's books

┼ ½ of Ete's books

If we now add 4 books, we have Pau's books (which the problem says is 32 books).

┼ Ete's books

┼ Pau's books (32 books)

   (4 more books)

┼ ½ of Ete's books

Step 2. To solve the problem work backwards. The diagram shows that if 4 books are taken from Pau he will have exactly one-half as many as Ete.

Pau's books − 4 = ½ of Ete's books

32 − 4 = 28 = ½ of Ete's books

Step 3. One-half the number of books owned by Ete is 28. So Ete owns twice this number.

Ete's books = 2 × 28 = 56

Step 4. Ete owns 56 books.

Problem 17

Leslie owns 1 more than 3 times as many dresses as Su. Leslie owns 28 dresses. How many dresses does Su own?

Note: Make a diagram in the space below if it helps your thinking.

Original Problem

>Leslie owns 1 more than 3 times as many dresses as Su. Leslie owns 28 dresses. How many dresses does Su own?

Problem Solution

Step 1. The relationship between the number of dresses owned by Su and by Leslie is shown in the diagram.

> ┼ Leslie's dresses
>
> │ 1 more dress
>
> ┼ 3 × Su's dresses
>
> │
>
> ┼ Su's dresses

Step 2. Leslie owns 28 dresses.

Step 3. Leslie owns one more than three times as many dresses as Su. So if one dress is taken from Leslie, she will have exactly three times as many dresses as Su.

$$\text{Leslie's dresses} - 1 = 3 \times \text{Su's dresses}$$
$$28 - 1 = 3 \times \text{Su's dresses}$$
$$27 = 3 \times \text{Su's dresses}$$

Step 4. Since 27 is three times as many dresses as Su owns, the number of dresses owned by Su can be obtained by dividing 27 by three.

$$\text{Su's dresses} = \frac{27}{3} = 9$$

Step 5. Su owns 9 dresses.

Problem 18

Jim's weekly income is $100.00 less than triple John's weekly income. Huey's weekly income is $20.00 more than double John's weekly income. Huey's income is $120.00. What is Jim's income?

Note: If you have difficulty you may find it helpful to follow these steps.

1. Diagram the relationship between John's and Huey's income.

2. Determine John's income.

3. Diagram the relationship between John's and Jim's income.

4. Determine Jim's income.

Original Problem

Jim's weekly income is $100.00 less than triple John's weekly income. Huey's weekly income is $20.00 more than double John's weekly income. Huey's income is $120.00. What is Jim's income?

Problem Solution *(Diagrams are shown below)*

Step 1. The problem asks for Jim's income. It gives Huey's income as $120.00 and it tells how to get John's income from Huey's income and then Jim's income from John's income.

Huey's income → John's income → Jim's income

Step 2. Huey's income is $120.00. This is $20.00 more than double John's income. So, if $20.00 is subtracted, it will be double John's income. (See diagram)

Huey's income − $20 = 2 × John's income
$120 − $20 = $100 = 2 × John's income

Step 3. Double John's income is $100.00, so John's income is one-half of $100.00.

$$\text{John's income} = \frac{\$100}{2} = \$50$$

Step 4. Jim's income is $100.00 less than triple John's weekly income. So triple John's income minus $100.00 is Jim's income. (See diagram)

3 × John's income − $100 = Jim's income
3 × $50 − $100 = Jim's income
$150 − $100 = Jim's income

Step 5. Jim's income is $50.00.

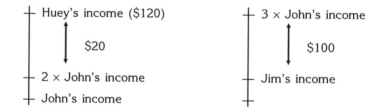

Problem 19

The sum of the weekly income of Bill and his wife, Rachel, is $1300.00 less than triple Xudy's income. Bill makes $400.00 less than double what his wife makes. Rachel makes $800.00. How much does Xudy make?

Original Problem

The sum of the weekly income of Bill and his wife, Rachel, is $1300.00 less than triple Xudy's income. Bill makes $400.00 less than double what his wife makes. Rachel makes $800.00. How much does Xudy make?

Problem Solution

Step 1. Bill's wife makes $800.00.

Wife—$800

Step 2. Bill makes $400.00 less than double what his wife makes. So Bill's income can be obtained by doubling Rachel's income and subtracting $400.00.

$$\text{Bill's income} = 2 \times \text{wife's} - \$400$$
$$\text{Bill's income} = 2 \times \$800 - \$400$$
$$\text{Bill's income} = \$1600 - \$400 = \$1200$$

Bill—$1200

Step 3. The sum of Bill's and his wife's income is $1300.00 less than triple Xudy's income.

Step 4. The sum of Bill's and his wife's income is: $1200 + $800 = $2000

Step 5. So $2000.00 is $1300.00 less than triple Xudy's income. This means that if $1300.00 is added to $2000.00 we will have triple Xudy's income.

$$\$1300 + \$2000 = 3 \times \text{Xudy's income}$$
$$\$3300 = 3 \times \text{Xudy's income}$$

Step 6. $3300.00 is triple Xudy's income. So Xudy's income can be obtained by dividing $3300.00 by 3.

$$\text{Xudy's income} = \frac{\$3300}{3} = \$1100$$

Step 7. Xudy's income is $1100.00.

Problem 20

Double Pete's weekly income is $50.00 less than the combined incomes of Joe and Sally. Patti, who makes $170.00 a week, makes $20.00 a week less than Sally but $40.00 more than Pete. How much does Joe make?

Original Problem

Double Pete's weekly income is $50.00 less than the combined incomes of Joe and Sally. Patti, who makes $170.00 a week, makes $20.00 a week less than Sally but $40.00 more than Pete. How much does Joe make?

Problem Solution

Step 1. The first sentence says that double Pete's income is $50.00 less than the combined incomes of Joe and Sally. This is shown in the following diagram.

```
┤  Joe & Sally
│  $50
┤  2 × Pete
```

Step 2. The second sentence says Patti, who makes $170.00 a week, makes $20.00 a week less than Sally.

```
┤  Joe & Sally        ┤  $190      Sally
│  $50                │            $20
┤  2 × Pete           ┤  $170      Patti
```

Step 3. The sentence also says Patti makes $40.00 more than Pete.

```
┤  Joe & Sally        ┤  $190      Sally
│  $50                │            $20
┤  2 × Pete           ┤  $170      Patti
                      │            $40
                      ┤  $130      Pete
```

Step 4. If Pete's income is $130.00 a week, then double his income must be $260.00. This fact is placed on the left diagram.

```
       ┬  Joe & Sally        $190 ┬  Sally
       │     $50                  │    $20
 $260  ┼  2 × Pete          $170 ┼  Patti
                                  │    $40
                             $130 ┼  Pete
```

Step 5. The diagram on the left now shows us that the combined income of Joe and Sally is $310.00.

```
 $310 ┬  Joe & Sally         $190 ┬  Sally
      │     $50                   │    $20
 $260 ┼  2 × Pete            $170 ┼  Patti
                                  │    $40
                             $130 ┼  Pete
```

Step 6. We know that Sally makes $190.00 a week. Therefore Joe must make: $310 − $190 = $120 a week.

Problem 21

A stone statue was divided into 5 parts and packed in crates for shipping. The 5 full crates together weighed a total of 520 lbs, whereas each crate weighed 20 lbs empty. How much did the statue itself weigh?

Original Problem

A stone statue was divided into 5 parts and packed in crates for shipping. The 5 full crates together weighed a total of 520 lbs, whereas each crate weighed 20 lbs empty. How much did the statue itself weigh?

Problem Solution

Step 1. Each empty crate weighs 20 pounds. Therefore the weight of 5 crates is:

$$
\begin{array}{r}
20 \\
\times\ 5 \\
\hline
100
\end{array}
$$

Step 2. The weight of the statue is the total weight minus the weight of the 5 crates.

$$
\begin{array}{r}
520 \\
-\ 100 \\
\hline
420
\end{array}
$$

The statue weighs 420 pounds.

Problem 22

A metal statue was divided into 5 parts and packed in crates for shipping. Each full crate weighed 520 lbs, whereas it weighed 20 lbs empty. How much did the statue itself weigh?

Original Problem

A metal statue was divided into 5 parts and packed in crates for shipping. Each full crate weighed 520 lbs, whereas it weighed 20 lbs empty. How much did the statue itself weigh?

Problem Solution

Step 1. Each crate weighed 520 pounds full and 20 pounds empty, so the weight of the piece of statue in each crate was:

$$
\begin{array}{r}
520 \\
-\ 20 \\
\hline
500
\end{array}
$$

Step 2. There were 5 pieces of statue each weighing 500 pounds, so the total weight of the statue was:

$$
\begin{array}{r}
500 \\
\times\ \ 5 \\
\hline
2500
\end{array}
$$

Problem 23

Paul sold 160 sandwiches for $2.00 each. Each sandwich consisted of 4 oz of ham, 2 slices of bread, and mustard. Paul paid $3.00 a pound for the ham, 60¢ a loaf for the bread (20 slices per loaf) and used 8 jars of mustard at 50¢ each. How much profit did he make?

Original Problem

Paul sold 160 sandwiches for $2.00 each. Each sandwich consisted of 4 oz of ham, 2 slices of bread, and mustard. Paul paid $3.00 a pound for the ham, 60¢ a loaf for the bread (20 slices per loaf) and used 8 jars of mustard at 50¢ each. How much profit did he make?

Problem Solution

Step 1. 160 sandwiches require 320 slices of bread.

Step 2. There are 20 slices of bread in a loaf, so the number of loaves is:

$$\begin{array}{r} 16 \\ 20\overline{)320} \end{array}$$

Step 3. The cost of 16 loaves of bread is:

$$\begin{array}{r} 16 \\ \times\,.60 \\ \hline 9.60 \text{ or } \$9.60 \end{array}$$

Step 4. 160 sandwiches require 640 ounces of ham.

Step 5. There are 16 ounces in a pound, so the number of pounds of ham is:

$$\begin{array}{r} 40 \\ 16\overline{)640} \end{array}$$

Step 6. The cost of 40 pounds of ham is:

$$\begin{array}{r} 3.00 \\ \times\quad 40 \\ \hline 120.00 \end{array}$$

Step 7. The cost of 8 jars of mustard at 50¢ each is:

$$\begin{array}{r} .50 \\ \times\; 8 \\ \hline 4.00 \end{array}$$

Step 8.   The total cost for bread, ham and mustard is:

$$
\begin{array}{r}
9.60 \\
120.00 \\
+\ \ \ 4.00 \\
\hline
133.60
\end{array}
$$

Step 9.   Paul sold 160 sandwiches for $2.00 each. So he collected:

$$
\begin{array}{r}
160 \\
\times\ \ \ 2.00 \\
\hline
320.00
\end{array}
$$

Step 10.   Paul's profit is the amount of money he collected minus the total cost:

$$
\begin{array}{r}
320.00 \\
-\ 133.60 \\
\hline
186.40
\end{array}
$$

Paul's profit is $186.40.

Problem 24

Ornamental chain sells for $1.23 a foot. How much will farmer Jones have to spend for chain in order to enclose a 70′ × 30′ patch of ground, leaving a 4′ entrance in the middle of each of the 30′ sides?

Original Problem

Ornamental chain sells for $1.23 a foot. How much will farmer Jones have to spend for chain in order to enclose a 70' × 30' patch of ground, leaving a 4' entrance in the middle of each of the 30' sides?

Problem Solution

Step 1. Farmer Jones' garden is shown below with the 4' entrances.

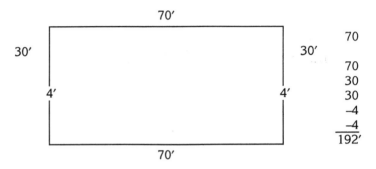

Step 2. The length of chain needed is 192 ft.
Therefore the cost is $1.23 × 192 = $236.16.

Note: The remaining problems require familiarity with some terms in mathematics and operations with fractions and powers. If you are unfamiliar with these topics but have developed the skill of careful, analytical thinking, you can learn them readily by taking a course in basic math in high school, college, or an adult education program. A good textbook in this area is *Developing Mathematical Skills: Computation, Problem Solving, and Basics for Algebra*, by Whimbey and Lochhead, McGraw Hill, Inc., 1981.

Problem 25

A certain ball, when dropped from any height, bounces one-third of the original height. If the ball is dropped from 54 ft, bounces back up, and continues to bounce up and down, what is the total distance that the ball has traveled when it hits the ground for the fourth time? Remember to count both the ascending and descending portions of the ball's path in computing the total distance.

Hint: make a diagram to represent the total path of the ball. You may want to show the ball bouncing at an angle, instead of straight up and down, in order to be able to see the ball's entire path. The beginning of such a diagram is shown below.

Original Problem

A certain ball, when dropped from any height, bounces one-third of the original height. If the ball is dropped from 54 ft, bounces back up, and continues to bounce up and down, what is the total distance that the ball has traveled when it hits the ground for the fourth time?

Problem Solution

Step 1. Ball drops from a height of 54 ft. So when it hits the ground it will have traveled 54 ft.

Step 2. The ball bounces back up one-third of 54 ft: 54/3 = 18.

So, at that point it has travelled a total of 54 + 18 = 72 ft.

Step 3. The ball continues to fall and bounces up one-third as high.

The first 4 bounces are shown in the following diagram. (Although the bounces may have been straight up, they are drawn slanted to the right so that they can all be seen.)

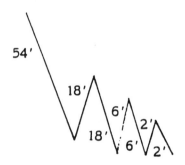

Step 4. How far will it have traveled when it hits the ground for the fourth time?

$$
\begin{array}{r}
54 \\
18 \\
18 \\
6 \\
6 \\
2 \\
\underline{2} \\
106
\end{array}
$$

The sum is 106 ft.

Problem 26

A car starts on a trip from city A to city B which is 60 miles away. It runs out of gas after it has gone one-third of the second half of the trip. How many miles still remain of the trip to city B?

Original Problem

> A car starts on a trip from city *A* to city *B* which is 60 miles away. It runs out of gas after it has gone one-third of the second half of the trip. How many miles still remain of the trip to city *B?*

Problem Solution

Step 1. The car ran out of gas after it went one-third of the second half of the trip. First the car went one-half of the trip. This is shown below.

Step 2. Then the car went one-third of the second half.

Step 3. The entire trip is 60 miles, so half the trip is 30 miles, and one-third of 30 miles is 10 miles.

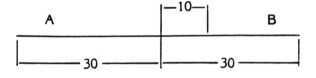

Step 4. How many miles still remain of the trip to city B? There are 20 miles remaining to city B.

Problem 27

If the sum of two positive whole numbers is 10, what is their greatest possible product?

Note: When two numbers are multiplied together, the answer is called the "product."

Original Problem

If the sum of two positive whole numbers is 10, what is their greatest possible product?

Problem Solution

Step 1. The column labeled SUM shows all combinations of positive whole numbers whose sum is 10.

The column labeled PRODUCT shows the product for each combination.

SUM	PRODUCT
1 + 9 = 10	1 × 9 = 9
2 + 8 = 10	2 × 8 = 16
3 + 7 = 10	3 × 7 = 21
4 + 6 = 10	4 × 6 = 24
5 + 5 = 10	5 × 5 = 25

Step 2. The product is largest when the two numbers are equal:

$$5 \times 5 = 25.$$

Problem 28

Is the sum of any two even positive integers—each of which is less than 10—odd or even?

Original Problem

Is the sum of any two even positive integers—each of which is less than 10—odd or even?

Problem Solution

Step 1. Here are the sums of all pairs of even positive integers, where each is less than 10:

$$2 + 4 = 6 \qquad 4 + 6 = 10$$
$$2 + 6 = 8 \qquad 4 + 8 = 12$$
$$2 + 8 = 10 \qquad 6 + 8 = 14$$

Step 2. All these sums are even.

See the end of this chapter for a more detailed discussion of this problem.

Problem 29

Which is bigger, *a* or *b*?

$$a = 4^2 5^3$$
$$b = 4^3 5^2$$

Note: 4^3 means $4 \times 4 \times 4$

$4^3 5^2$ means $4 \times 4 \times 4 \times 5 \times 5$

Original Problem

> Which is bigger, *a* or *b*? $a = 4^2 5^3$
> $b = 4^3 5^2$

Problem Solution

Step 1. a = 4 × 4 × 5 × 5 × 5

b = 4 × 4 × 4 × 5 × 5

Step 2. These products can be rewritten like this:

a (4 × 4 × 5 × 5) × 5

b (4 × 4 × 5 × 5) × 4

Step 3. This shows that a is bigger.

Problem 30

Which is bigger, *a* or *b*?

$$a = 2^5 4^3 7^6$$
$$b = 2^6 4^4 7^5$$

Original Problem

Which is bigger, a or b?

$$a = 2^5 4^3 7^6$$
$$b = 2^6 4^4 7^5$$

Problem Solution

Step 1. Note that $7^6 = 7^5 \times 7$.

Therefore: $a = 2^5 4^3 7^6 = 2^5 4^3 7^5 \times 7$

Step 2. Note that $2^6 = 2 \times 2^5$ and $4^4 = 4 \times 4^3$.

Therefore: $b = 2^6 4^4 7^5 = 2 \times 2^5 \times 4 \times 4^3 \times 7^5 = 2^5 4^3 7^5 \times 2 \times 4$

Step 3. We now have: $a = 2^5 4^3 7^5 \times 7$
$b = 2^5 4^3 7^5 \times 2 \times 4$
or
$b = 2^5 4^3 7^5 \times 8$

Step 4. This shows that b is larger.

Problem 31

Here is how a number is multiplied by a fraction:

$$3 \times \frac{1}{35} = \frac{3 \times 1}{35} = \frac{3}{35}$$

$$3 \times \frac{2}{35} = \frac{3 \times 2}{35} = \frac{6}{35}$$

$$5 \times \frac{2}{35} = \frac{5 \times 2}{35} = \frac{\overset{1}{\cancel{5}} \times 2}{\underset{7}{\cancel{35}}} = \frac{2}{7}$$

Using this procedure, multiply 5^2 times $\dfrac{1}{4^7 5^3}$

Original Problem

Multiply 5^2 times $\dfrac{1}{4^7 5^3}$

Problem Solution

$$5^2 \times \frac{1}{4^7 5^3} = \frac{5^2}{4^7 5^3} = \frac{5 \times 5}{4^7 \times 5 \times 5 \times 5} = \frac{\overset{1}{\cancel{5}} \times \overset{1}{\cancel{5}}}{4^7 \times \underset{1}{\cancel{5}} \times \underset{1}{\cancel{5}} \times 5} = \frac{1}{4^7 5}$$

ADDITIONAL PROBLEMS

1. In the time a car travels 4 mi, a plane travels 30 mi. When the car travels 60 mi, how far does the plane travel?

2. Tarzan can swim 8 ft in the time a crocodile swims 10 ft. When Tarzan swims 20 ft, how far does the crocodile swim?

3. Paul can run 12 ft in the time Bob runs 10 ft.
   a. When Paul runs 6 ft, how far does Bob run? _____ ft
   b. When Paul runs 3 ft, how far does Bob run? _____ ft
   c. When Paul runs 30 ft, how far does Bob run? _____ ft
   d. When Paul runs 246 ft, how far does Bob run? _____ ft

4. A restaurant uses 2 pt of milk with 3 pt of cream to make coffee creamer. To make a larger quantity of the mixture, how many pints of cream should they use with 18 pt of milk?

5. A warped 12-in ruler is only 11 in long. Unaware of this, Judy used the ruler to measure off 48 in of rope. What was the true length of the rope?

6. A 5-in piece of cloth shrank to 4 in when it was washed. At that rate, how long would a 75-in piece of cloth measure after washing?

7. A clock runs fast. It says 8 min have passed when only 5 min have passed. How much time has really passed when the clock says 20 min have passed?

8. Yvette makes $20.00 a week less than double Celeste. Yvette makes $320.00 a week. How much does Celeste make?

9. Bob and Fred together make $20.00 a week less than double John. John makes $110.00 a week and Bob makes $140.00 a week. How much does Fred make?

10. Dero makes $70.00 a week more than double Willie. Also, Dero makes $15.00 a week less than Harry. Harry makes $185.00. How much does Willie make?

11. Beverly makes $25.00 less than Jody and Hal combined. Jody makes $30.00 less than Hal. Hal makes $140.00. How much does Beverly make?

12. If Joe's weekly income doubled he would be making $70.00 a week more than Joan. Joe's weekly income is $20.00 more than one-half of Bill's. Bill makes $200.00 a week. How much does Joan make?

13. If Tommy had three more books he would have twice as many as Helen. Tommy has 21 books. How many does Helen have?

14. The number of dresses owned by Beth is the number owned by Julie divided by the number owned by J. E. Julie, who owns 28 dresses, would own five times as many dresses as J. E. if she had 7 more dresses. How many dresses does Beth have?

15. Jack weighs 25 lbs less than Phil. Bill weighs 40 lbs more than Jack. Frank weighs 70 lbs less than Bill. Al weighs 5 lbs less than Frank. Which man is heaviest? Which is lightest?

16. Starting at one end of my street, my house is the third house. Starting at the other end, my house is the seventh one. Not counting my house, how many houses are on my side of the street?

17. Starting at one end of a street, the police station is the fifth building. Starting at the other end, it is the ninth building. Including the police station, how many buildings are on that side of the street?

18. Fred and Tom attended the same school. Fred lives 7 mi away and Tom lives 9 mi away.

    a. What is the greatest possible distance between their homes?

    b. What is the shortest possible distance between their homes?

19. There are 15 books stacked in a single pile. How many books are between 2 other books?

Some of the following problems require familiarity with concepts and operations in mathematics such as fractions, decimals, percents, area, coordinates, negative numbers, and powers. If you are unfamiliar with these topics but have developed the skill of careful, analytical thinking, you can learn them by taking a course in basic mathematics in high school, college, or an adult education program. These problems are included here to show you the types of questions you may encounter on standardized academic aptitude tests.

20. A certain ball, when dropped from any height, bounces one-half the original height. If it was dropped from 80 ft and allowed to bounce freely, what was the total distance it traveled when it hit the ground for the third time?

21. A mouse made a dash from the cellar door to his hole in the living room wall which was 90 ft away. The cat saw him after he had gone one-third of the second half of the distance. How far did the mouse still have to run for safety? Make a diagram showing the distances.

22. A car started on a trip from city X to city Y which is 120 mi away. It ran out of gas one-quarter of the way through the last third of the trip. How many miles did it travel before running out of gas?

23. Is the sum of any two positive odd integers—each of which is less than 10—odd or even? (See pages 332–333 for a detailed solution.)

24. Is the sum of any odd and even positive integers—each of which is less than 10—odd or even?

25. Is the sum of any 2 consecutive positive integers—each of which is less than 10—odd, even, or either?

26. Is the sum of any 3 consecutive positive integers—each of which is less than 10—odd, even, or either?

27. Is the sum of any 4 consecutive positive integers—each of which is less than 10—odd, even, or either?

28. Is the sum of any 5 consecutive positive integers—each of which is less than 10—odd, even, or either?

29. If the product of 2 positive equal numbers is 25, what is their sum?

30. A rectangular park is .6 mile long and .5 mile wide.

    a. What is the area of the park? (Area = Length × Width)

    b. What is the perimeter of the park? (The perimeter is the total distance around the park.)

31. A square park is 1.5 mi long on each side.

    a. What is the area of the park?

    b. What is the perimeter of the park?

32. If the area of a rectangular park is 30 square mi and the width of the park is .5 mi, what is the length?

33. If the perimeter of a square park is 1.2 square mi, what is the length of each side?

34. A square is 3 ft long on each side. A rectangle is 2 ft long and 7 ft wide. What is the ratio of the perimeter of the square to the perimeter of the rectangle?

35. One square is 6 in long on each side. Another square has sides which are only one-half as long. What is the ratio of the area of the small square to the large square?

36. Eighty-eight pounds of a medicine was divided into 1000 equal parts. How much did each part weigh?

37. Fred bought a car for $4000.00 and sold it 2 years later for 70% of what he paid.

    a. How much did he sell it for?

    b. How much less did he sell it for than he paid for it?

38. A dealer bought a TV for $300.00, then sold it for 40% more than that price.

   a. How much profit did he make?

   b. How much did he sell it for?

39. An art dealer bought a painting for $500.00 and sold it 2 years later for 350% of the price he paid. How much did he sell it for?

40. The line below is marked off into 4 equal parts. If you start at point A and go 70% of the way to point E, between which 2 letters would you be? *Hint:* ¼ equals 25%.

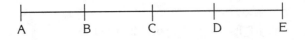

41. a. The line below is marked off into 5 equal parts. If you start at point U and go 150% of the distance to point V, between which two letters would you be?

   b. If you start at point U and go 380% of the distance to point V, between which two letters would you be?

42. a. Which is bigger, *a* or *b*?

   $a = 2^5 4^4 7^6$

   $b = 2^6 4^4 7^5$

   b. Which is bigger, *a* or *b*?

   $a = 2^7 3^6 7^9$

   $b = 2^9 3^7 7^8$

43. Perform each multiplication and reduce the answer to simplest terms.

    a. Multiply 20 times $\dfrac{1}{200}$

    b. Multiply 30 times $\dfrac{1}{900}$

    c. Multiply 5^3 times $\dfrac{1}{5^2}$

    d. Multiply 5^2 times $\dfrac{1}{5^3}$

    e. Multiply 5^3 times $\dfrac{1}{5^3}$

    f. Multiply 5^3 times $\dfrac{1}{5^3 4^2}$

44. Monthly Utility Bills For The Jones' In 1998

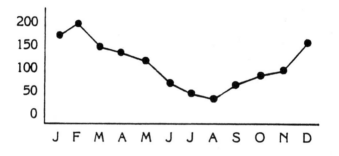

    a. Is the average of the monthly utility bills more or less than $150.00?

    b. Is the average of the monthly utility bills for January and February more or less than the total of the bills for November and December?

    c. How much higher was the utility bill in January than in June?

45. *a.* How many faces does the cube shown below have?

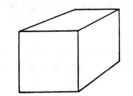

    b. If each edge of the cube is 6 in long, how many square inches of paper are required to cover all faces of the cube?

46. *a.* If the cube below is cut in half along the dotted line, how many total faces do the two pieces have?

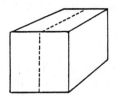

    b. If each edge of the original cube was 6 in long, how many square inches of paper would be required to cover all the faces of the two pieces produced by cutting the cube?

47. *a.* If the cube below is cut into quarters along the dotted lines, how many total faces do the four pieces have?

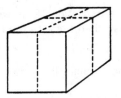

    b. If each edge of the original cube was 6 in long, how many square inches of paper would be required to cover all the faces of the four pieces produced by cutting the cube?

48. A company bought 60 gallons of soda for $30.00 and quart-size bottles for 5¢ each. How much total profit did they make if they sold all the soda for 50¢ a bottle? (One gallon equals 4 quarts.)

49. A garden is 50 ft long and 25 ft wide. How many total fence posts would be required to place a fence post at each corner and additional fence posts every 5 ft?

50. A field is 1500 ft long and 60 ft wide. How many total fence posts would be required to place a fence post at each corner and additional fence posts every 5 ft?

51. Mr. Smith's garden is 30 ft long and 21 ft wide and he would like to put a chain fence around it. The chain costs $5.00 a yard. He will support the chain by putting a metal post in each of the 4 corners and additional posts every 3 ft. The posts cost $2.00 each. What is the total cost of the chain and posts?

52. Starting at one corner, a park runs 30 mi east, 15 mi north, 10 mi east, 25 mi south, 40 mi west, then back to the first corner.

    a. Make a diagram of the park.

    b. Compute the distance around the park. (This distance is called the perimeter.)

53. Compute the area of the park described in problem 52 by dividing it into two rectangles and computing each part separately, then adding the two parts.

54. Starting at one corner, a park runs 10 mi west, 8 mi south, 20 mi west, 18 mi north, 30 mi east, then back to the first corner.

    a. Make a diagram of the park.

    b. Compute the distance around the park.

55. Compute the area of the park described in problem 54 by dividing it into two rectangles and computing each part separately, then adding the two parts.

56. John had $4000.00 in the bank on January 1, 1990. Each year for the next several years he spent 1/2 of the money he had in the bank at the beginning of the year. How much did he have in the bank on January 1, 1995?

57. Phil had $540.00 in the bank on January 1, 1991. Each year for the next several years he spent 1/3 of the money he had in the bank at the beginning of the year. How much did he have in the bank on January 1, 1994?

58. Phil had $540.00 in the bank on January 1, 1991. Each year for the next several years he spent 1/3 of the money he had in the bank at the beginning of the year. How much had he spent by January 1, 1994?

59. Jane deposited $2000.00 in an account which paid 10% interest per year. At the end of the first year she left the original $2000.00 and the interest in the account. How much was in the account at the end of the second year?

60.

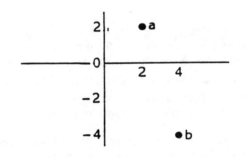

a. What are the coordinates of the point a? What are the coordinates of the point b?

b. Compute the distance between points a and b using this formula:

$$distance = \sqrt{(x_b - x_a)^2 + (y_b - y_a)^2}$$

61. If x − 8 is a positive number and x is a whole number, what is the smallest possible value of x?

62. If x + 7 is a negative number and x is an integer, what is the largest possible value of x?

63. If 5(2 + 1) = 20 + x, what is x?

64. If r is the radius of a circle and d is the diameter, which is larger:

$$r^2 \text{ or } \frac{d^2}{3}$$

65. If x − 7 = y + 9, which is larger, x or y?

Discussion for Problems 23–28

New knowledge in mathematics often results from a mathematician seeing a consistency and then showing theoretically why the consistency occurs. The process is similar to the steps you might use in solving this problem.

Is the sum of any two even integers odd or even?

Solution

Step 1. We will try adding several pairs of even integers to see if the sums are odd or even. We attempt to avoid using only special cases for which a conclusion might be true even though it is not true for all cases.

Experimenting with a few concrete cases is a good way to start many math problems involving general formulas or statements.

2 + 2 = 4	2 + 18 = 20	64 + 100 = 164
−10 + 16 = 6	−18 + −50 = −68	0 + 14 = 14

Step 2. All these sums are even numbers, so it appears that the sum of any two even integers is even.

Step 3. To be sure that the sum of any pair of even integers is even, we will begin with the definition of an even integer.

When an even integer is divided by 2 the answer is an integer, not a fraction or a mixed number.

This means that if A and B are any even integers, then:

$\dfrac{A}{2}$ is an integer $\dfrac{B}{2}$ is an integer

Step 4. We want to show that if A and B are even integers, then their sum (A + B) is also an even integer.

This means we must show that $\dfrac{A+B}{2}$ is an integer, not a fraction or a mixed number.

Step 5. From the rule for adding fractions we know that:

$$\frac{A+B}{2} = \frac{A}{2} + \frac{B}{2}$$

Step 6. We know that $\dfrac{A}{2}$ and $\dfrac{B}{2}$ are both integers.

Also, the sum of two integers is itself an integer.

Therefore, $\dfrac{A+B}{2}$ is an integer.

Step 7. This shows that the sum of any two even integers is also an even integer.

Here are some other problems that could be approached in the same way. Just remember that when 1 is divided by 2 the answer is ½, when −1 is divided by 2 the answer is − ½, and when other odd numbers are divided by 2 the answer is a mixed number with the fraction portion equal to ½. Furthermore, ½ + ½ = 1.

Is the sum of any two odd integers odd or even?

Is the sum of any odd and even integer odd or even?

Is the sum of any two consecutive integers odd or even?

Is the sum of any three consecutive integers odd, even, or either?

XII. THE POST-WASI TEST

Introduction

If you have diligently worked through all the exercises in this book, your analytical reading and reasoning skills should be appreciably sharper. You have probably noticed this already while reading technical material or solving problems. The test on the following pages is similar to the one you took at the beginning of the book. You will probably find, as do most people, that you can now deal with these questions more effectively and attain a higher score.

1. Which word is different from the other 3 words?

   a. water   b. ice   c. frozen   d. steam

2. Which letter is as far away from *P* in the alphabet as *M* is from *H*?

   a. *J*   b. *T*   c. *U*   d. *V*

3. If you are facing north and turn right, then make an about-face and turn right again, which direction is behind you?

4. Which pair of words fits best in the blanks?

   Bracelet is to wrist as _____ is to _____.

   a. neck : necklace   b. painting : wall
   c. hair : ribbon   d. jewelry : decoration

5. *3* is related to *2* as *60* is related to _____.

   a. 50   b. 20   c. 30   d. 40

6. Which set of letters is different from the other 3 sets?

    a. JKJI   b. GFGH   c. POPQ   d. NMNO

7. In a different language *peq bo* means "green book," *sa bo mai* means "green old house," and *ja mai* means "old man." What is the word for house in this language?

8. Write the 2 letters which should appear next in the series.

$$S\ T\ Q\ R\ U\ P\ M\ \_\_\ \_\_$$

9. Marcia is taller than Phil but shorter than Jack. Regarding the occupations in which these people are engaged, the electrician is the shortest, the cashier is the tallest, and the accountant is intermediate. What is Marcia's occupation?

10. A car ran out of gas one-third of the way through the second fifth of a 600-mile trip. How far had it traveled before running out of gas?

11. Which number in the following series is incorrect?

    12 8 15 11 17 14 21 17 24 20

    a. 11   b. 17   c. 18   d. 14

12. The first figure is related to the second figure in the same way that the third figure is related to one of the answer choices. Pick the answer.

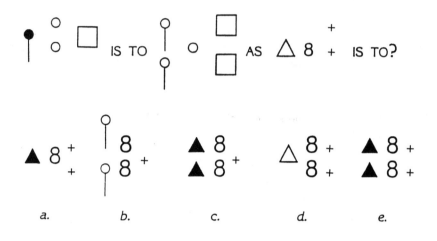

13. Which pair of words best fits the meaning of the sentence?

The man was angry, _____ he was _____ with the child.

a. but—rough   b. but—gentle
c. so—gentle   d. nevertheless—rough

14. Write the 3 numbers which should appear next in the series.

284 280 140 136 68 64 32 28 14 ___ ___ ___

15. A cardiologist is a _____ specialist.

a. brain   b. heart   c. ear and throat   d. lung   e. bone

16. Calligraphy pertains to:

    a. minerals   b. penmanship
    c. supernatural   d. Egypt

17. Pat makes $30.00 less than Jim and Mike combined. Pat makes $500.00 and Mike makes $210.00. How much does Jim make?

18. Which letter is in the same position in the alphabet as the letter *s* is in *comprehension*?

    a. c   b. j   c. a   d. i   e. none of the above

19. A tower always has _____.

    a. doors   b. windows   c. metal   d. width

20. Circle the letter before the letter in the word diction which occupies the same position in the word as it does in the name of the 9th month.

21. Which pair of words is different from the other 3 pairs?

    a. talk—fast   b. smile—laugh
    c. eat—heartily   d. look—carefully

22. The top 4 figures form a series which changes in a systematic manner according to some rule. Try to discover the rule and choose from among the alternatives the figure which should occur next in the series.

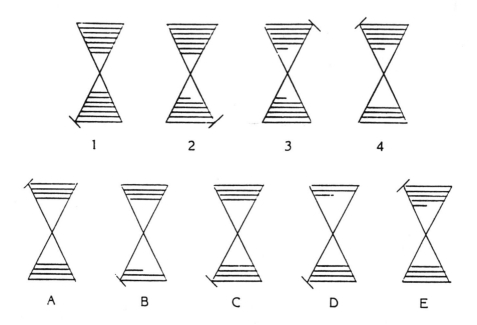

1   2   3   4

A   B   C   D   E

23. Which number is repeated first in the following series?

6 3 8 1 2 9 7 4 5 8 5 1 3 7 9 4 2 4

24. Which pair of words fits best in the blanks?

Room is to door as _____ is to _____.

a. entrance : exit   b. stairs : building
c. bottle : cap   d. rug : floor

25. Write the 3 pairs of letters which should come next.

    cY eV gW iT kU mR oS qP ___ ___ ___

26. One-half is related to 8 as 5 is related to _____.

    a. 20   *b.* 10   *c.* 75   *d.* 80

27. Forest is to tree as _____ is to _____.

    a. family : parents   *b.* plant : roots
    c. tree : leaves   *d.* tribe : Indian

28. Which word means the opposite of *ostracize?*

    a. expel   *b.* welcome   *c.* point   *d.* relevant

29. Which set of letters is different from the other 3 sets?

    a. AJKC   *b. LPQN*   *c. GBCH*   *d. SIJU*

30. Umbrella is to wet as _____ is to _____.

    a. sunshine : rain   *b.* coat : warm
    c. napkin : dirty   *d.* boots : feet

31. A car travels 30 miles in the time a boat travels 20 miles. How far does
    the car travel when the boat travels 90 miles?

    a. 60   *b.* 100   *c.* 135   *d.* 125

32. Alloy is to iron _____ as is to _____.

    a. metal : steel   *b.* chord : middle C
    c. B flat : C sharp   *d.* copper : bronze

33. How many fifths are there in 45/3?

    a. 3   *b.* 1   *c.* 60   *d.* 75

34. If 3 days before tomorrow is Friday, what is the day after tomorrow?

    _____

35. Which word is different from the other 3 words?

    a. pernicious   *b.* noxious   *c.* palliative   *d.* detrimental

36. 5 9 3 8 4 1 2 6. If the fourth number is larger than the seventh number, add the second number to the fifth number; otherwise add the first number of the eighth number. Either way, add the second number to your sum unless the seventh number is smaller than the third number. In that case add the fifth number. Write your answer here.

    _____

37. Select the answer which is most nearly equivalent in meaning to the following statement.

Wise men learn more from fools than fools from the wise.

    a. Knaves and fools divide the world.

    b. It is easier to be wise for others than for ourselves.

    c. He gains wisdom in a happy way, who gains it by another's experience.

    d. Accuracy of statement is one of the elements of truth; inaccuracy is a near kin to falsehood.

38. Nostalgia is to anticipation _____ as is to _____.

     a. present : past   *b.* future : past
     c. past : future   *d.* future : present

    After you have completed the test and checked your answers, you may want to go back and rework problems in the book which are similar to any that you missed.

XIII. MEETING ACADEMIC AND WORKPLACE STANDARDS: HOW THIS BOOK CAN HELP

Preparing for Academic Tests

Since the first publication of *Problem Solving and Comprehension* 20 years ago, a great deal has changed in education and in our understanding of mental processes. This chapter reviews connections between Thinking Aloud Pair Problem Solving (TAPPS), and the objectives described in recent educational framework and standard documents. Specifically, we show which framework objectives TAPPS will help you meet, and how and which parts of the major assessments can be prepared for with the Sixth Edition of *Problem Solving Comprehension*.

National Mathematics Standards

The NCTM Curriculum and Evaluation Standards (NCTM, 1989, pp. 5–6) describes five goals as being essential for attaining mathematical literacy:

1. Learning to value mathematics.
2. Becoming confident in one's own ability.
3. Becoming a mathematical problem solver.
4. Learning to communicate mathematically.
5. Learning to reason mathematically.

These are precisely the outcomes of the TAPPS process when it is applied to solving math problems.

The Standards state that "students need extensive experience listening to, reading about, writing about, speaking about, reflecting on, and demonstrating mathematical ideas. . . . It is not enough for students to write the answer to an exercise or even to 'show all their steps.' It is equally important that students be able to describe how they reach an answer or the difficulties they encountered while trying to solve a problem" (p. 140). TAPPS develops mathematical communication skills as no other instructional method can. By requiring a detailed description of each reasoning step, TAPPS builds reasoning skills while it fosters an extraordinarily deep level of mathematical communication. Yet it does this starting at the learners' level by demanding that the problem solver and listener understand each other. This is in marked contrast to traditional approaches that demand communication according to some externally directed format (whether two-column proof or portfolio-style log book) designed to meet the needs of the teacher or some distant authority. Externally mandated structures are never as meaningful or as rigorous as those imposed by the dynamics of the problem solver–listener interaction. Because the listener is constantly monitoring and probing the problem solver's thinking, a level of explicitness and an awareness of detail can be attained that goes far beyond that required in written proofs or other standard forms of mathematical communication.

As reasoning and communication skills improve, learners acquire a more sophisticated ability in solving problems and this in turn creates a genuine confidence based on a realistic awareness of actual accomplishments. Finally, given confidence in their skills, learners can begin to build an honest sense for the value of mathematics in their own lives.

Alignment of Whimbey and Lochhead: *Problem Solving and Comprehension*
With the NCTM *Curriculum And Evaluation Standards For School Mathematics*

NCTM Standards	Problem Solving and Comprehension
Becoming Confident In One's Own Ability	*This Is the Purpose of the Entire Book*
Becoming A Mathematical Problem Solver • Use with increasing confidence problem solving approaches to investigate and understand mathematical content. • Analyze the situation in light of their existing knowledge, develop appropriate techniques, and subsequently apply those techniques to solve the problem. • Recognizing and formulating their own problems.	• Description of problem solver (pp. 26–27). • Problems and solutions offered in chapter III model problem solving through step-by-step analysis and deductive reasoning. • A varied array of visual representation of problems is also part of the presentation of solutions. • Problems 38–40 (pp. 125–130) combine problem solving skills with basic numerical operations. • Formulating own problems (pp. 40–41). • Work in chapters VI and VII develops appropriate strategies and techniques and subsequently applies those techniques to solve the problems, using multiple representations of ideas including verbal, numerical, symbolic, and a combination of all in chapter VIII. • Chapter XI: Solving Mathematical Word Problems contextualizes the skills and strategies developed to this point. Provides a good balance of concrete and abstract problems, requiring the application of problem solving, reasoning, and computational skills, along with skills of communications and visual representations.

Learning To Communicate Mathematically

- Describe how they reach an answer or the difficulties they encountered while trying to solve a problem.
- Clarify, paraphrase, and elaborate on problems.
- Mathematical communication becomes more formal and symbolic.
- Thinking mathematically, solving problems, and reflecting on one's own mathematical experiences.
- Techniques of writing mathematics should emphasize brainstorming, clarifying, and revising as applied to problem solving.
- Reflect on and clarify their thinking about mathematical ideas and relationships.
- Formulate mathematical definitions and express generalizations discovered through investigations.
- Express mathematical ideas orally and in writing.
- Read written presentations of mathematics with understanding.
- Ask clarifying and extending questions related to mathematics they have read or heard about.
- Appreciate the economy, power, and elegance of mathematical notation and its role in the development of mathematical ideas.

- Multiple representation of listening skills in several examples (pp. 23–25, 29–39)
- Description of listener (pp. 28–29)
- In problems 1 to 4 (pp. 43–50), the concept of transitivity is explored, using a single variable and a simple linear diagram—basically a line graph, to capture the relationships embedded in the words.
- Problems 5 to 8 (pp. 51–61) make use of two variables, and present newer sources of information. Not all information is numerical or even quantitative. The use of tables as visual and conceptual organizer is introduced.

345

Alignment of Whimbey and Lochhead: *Problem Solving and Comprehension*
With the *NCTM Curriculum And Evaluation Standards For School Mathematics*

NCTM Standards	Problem Solving and Comprehension
Learning To Reason Mathematically	
• Follow logical arguments. • Generalizing from a pattern of observations. • Test the conjecture (deductive reasoning, verification). • Expand the role of reasoning. • Have numerous and varied experiences with proof and proof technique. • Experience numerical patterns.	• Checking methods and verifying results are embedded in the methods (chapter III). • Deductive reasoning modeled in examples (pp. 29–39). • The concepts are presented in multiple perspectives, and in increasing levels of complexity and abstraction (chapter III). • Noticing patterns (induction) in combination with deduction is used to derive answers in problems 36 and 37 (pp. 119–124). • Problems 17 to 24 lead students to greater formalization and abstraction, where the visual representation or the symbolization of relationships is the end in itself, not the means to the end of finding a solution to a specific problem. This higher level of formal understanding is applied in problems 25 to 28, using both qualitative and quantitative variables (pp. 97–104). • Problems 11 and 12 make use of counterfactuals to derive data and transfer this method in instructions to problem 13 (pp. 67–72).

Making Mathematical Connections

- Recognize equivalent representations of the same concept.
- Apply and translate different representations of the same problem situation or of the same mathematical concept.
- Modeling connections between problem situations and their mathematical representations.
- Mathematical connections between two equivalent representations and corresponding processes in each.
- Look back at the solution process to consider other possible strategies.

- Problems 9 and 10 (pp. 63–66) make use of multiple representations of the same problem by different organization of the same information into tables and checklists
- Problems 15 and 16 combine and integrate several of the preceding approaches, including relational diagrams, making use of non-numerical data and relationships, and deduction (pp. 75–79).
- Problems 25–28 use both qualitative and quantitative variables (pp. 97–104).
- Chapter X: Deductive and Hypothetical Thinking Through Days of the Week unfolds an application of problem solving, sequencing, deductive and inductive reasoning using a real world set of seemingly non-quantitative symbols: the days of the week. They are symbols for a cyclic set of numbers. These problems use skills in a new context
- Chapter XI: Solving Mathematical Word Problems connects skills covered in previous chapters to the solving of mathematical word problems.

National Science Standards

The *National Science Education Standards* (NRC, 1996) also called for an approach to instruction that was well aligned with the benefits of TAPPS. According to these Standards, "inquiry" is the key component in science learning and "inquiry requires the identification of assumptions, use of critical and logical thinking, and consideration of alternative explanations" (p. 23). These are precisely the skills that the TAPPS dynamic demands and develops.

In describing how to teach the skills of inquiry, the Standards ask teachers to "orchestrate discourse among students about science ideas" (p. 36). Without being very specific about how this can be done, the Standards outline the following:

> An important stage of inquiry and of student science learning is the oral and written discourse that focuses the attention of students on how they know what they know and how their knowledge connects to larger ideas, other domains, and the world beyond the classroom. Teachers directly support and guide this discourse in two ways: They require students to record their work—teaching the necessary skills as appropriate—and they promote many different forms of communication (for example, spoken, written, pictorial, graphic, mathematical and electronic). Using a collaborative group structure, teachers encourage interdependency among group members, assisting students to work together in small groups so that all participate in sharing data and in developing group reports. Teachers also give groups opportunities to make presentations of their work and to engage with their classmates in explaining, clarifying, and justifying what they have learned. (p. 36)

These objectives will not happen simply because the National Academy of Science says they should. Small group discussions do not spontaneously gravitate to the consideration of how we know what we know or to a rigorous analysis of basic assumptions. Specific instructional structures are needed to encourage these outcomes and to help refine first (inevitably inadequate) efforts. The advantage that TAPPS has over other structures is that it creates a **natural dynamic** in which learners are responsible for these outcomes while teachers are free to monitor the big picture, to coach specific pairs who may be in need of assistance, and to insure that the overall inquiry attains its scientific objectives. By creating a learner-based dynamic to drive the search for an even greater precision of detail, TAPPS insures that inquiry becomes a learning activity rather than a teacher mandated process to which students reluctantly conform. Because *Problem Solving and Comprehension* provides a prerequisite preparation for the Science Standards we do not include a detailed table relating specific problems to individual standards.

National Standards for Reading and Writing

There is currently no politically acceptable consensus on national standards for reading and writing. A wide gap remains between many current educational theories and effective educational practice. This situation is particularly tragic given the enormous importance of these skills and the number of highly effective strategies that have been developed and exhaustively tested during the past two decades (e.g., Clay, 1987; Linden & Whimbey, 1990b; Whimbey, Johnson, Williams, & Linden, 1993).

Both reading and writing are highly complex skills that demand a great deal of experience and judgment. The composition or interpretation of text rarely can be accomplished through a few simple rules. That is why these skills have remained, and will continue to remain, beyond the realm of computers. Yet these complex skills depend on a number of simpler skills that can and must be fully developed. Thus, for example, the ability to compose a coherent paragraph contains, as one component, the skill of arranging a set of sentences in their most meaningful order. These skills can and should be practiced separately from the more complex activities in which they are eventually practiced.

Problem Solving and Comprehension teaches a few of the most important skills needed in reading and writing: step by step analysis, structural diagramming of relationships and sequences, and the structure and function of analogies. Additional skills are contained in *The Whimbey Writing Program* (Whimbey & Blanton, 1995), and in *Analytical Reading and Reasoning* (Whimbey, 1989).

The most important contribution of *Problem Solving and Comprehension* to the development of literacy is not in the specific skills it teaches, but in the strategy of TAPPS. A very similar strategy is at the heart of Reading Recovery (Clay, 1985, 1991, 1993), one of the most carefully researched education programs of all time. In this highly effective program the teacher takes on a role similar to that of the listener while the student-reader performs the role of the problem solver. Reading Recovery uses this strategy in teaching, staff training, and reading research. Another successful approach, Reciprocal Reading (Brown & Palincsar, 1989) employs a variant in which students perform roles analogous to those of the listener and problem solver. TAPPS is the least difficult strategy of the three to implement and the most adaptable to scaling up for use with large numbers of teachers and students. It is the only one of the strategies primarily designed for use in high school and beyond. It is the approach which places the greatest degree of responsibility and control in the hands of the learners. More specific descriptions of the role of TAPPS in the development of reading and writing competence can be found in *Blueprint for Educational Change: Improving Reasoning, Literacies, and Science Achievement with Cooperative Learning* (Whimbey et al., 1993) and in *Why Johnny Can't Write* (Linden & Whimbey, 1990b).

All of the standards for reading, writing, mathematics, and science base their recommendations on the results of cognitive research into thinking and learning processes. In the next section we examine how *Problem Solving and Comprehension* relates to that body of research.

A Few Lessons from Cognitive Science

Modern cognitive psychology is, in many respects, a direct consequence of the digital computer. The existence of computer programs provide psychologists with a tangible model for the mental processes earlier Behaviorist Psychologists had no means for imagining. Despite cognitive psychology's recent origins, important educational implications have been apparent for 15 years. In her Presidential address to the 1987 AERA convention, Lauren Resnick summarized some of those implications. Resnick indicated that the most effective programs for teaching thinking share three characteristics:

1. They involve socially shared intellectual work, and they are organized around joint accomplishment of tasks, so that elements of the skill take on meaning in the context of the whole.

2. They make usually hidden processes overt, and they encourage student observation and commentary. They also allow skill to build up bit by bit, yet permit participation even for the relatively unskilled.

3. Most successful programs are organized around particular bodies of knowledge and interpretation—subject matter . . . rather than general abilities. The treatment of the subject matter is tailored to engage students in processes of meaning construction and interpretation. (Resnick, 1987)

The TAPPS process clearly fits all aspects of the first two characteristics. No other program is as effective in making usually hidden processes overt. According to Resnick's third criterion, our application of TAPPS to test preparation could be criticized as too narrowly focused on general abilities. In fact, the most successful applications of *Problem Solving and Comprehension* have been those that use the text in a program focused on a specific subject matter, such as mathematics, chemistry, or English composition. We designed the book to be a short course in analytical reasoning, because we do not believe a long course would be as effective. When using *Problem Solving and Comprehension* keep in mind that this text was not intended to be used in isolation and that it is very important for you to extend the lessons learned to at least one specific subject matter content.

The Importance of Unimportant Contexts

Cognitive science has repeatedly revealed the importance of context. Knowledge gained in one context is not usually transferred automatically, making it useful in a second related context. From this, many educators have concluded that all skills need to be learned within a specific real-world application. In addition, the desire to make education more engaging for students encourages the use of applied problems and the avoidance of abstract or meaningless situations. Yet in this book you will find very few real-world problems. In most cases the problems deal with silly situations in which no one could ever have a really serious interest. Why is this?

This course is designed to help you improve your skills in analytical reasoning. Cognitive science has shown that emotions are often a great obstacle to clear-headed analytical thinking. When we are deeply concerned, excited, or fearful, special hormones, such as adrenaline, kick in and affect the way we think. Whenever we care strongly about the outcome of a process, our attention is focused more on some aspects of the problem than on others. We distort information to give some data special importance. These distortions can be very useful. If, for example, you are being tracked by a tiger in the jungle, it is important that you pay attention to the tiger and not to the insects that may be biting you. But distorted attention is not useful in tests or in situations where it is important to consider all the data. Controlled emotion, a passion for success, is, of course, the key to any excellent performance. But for the TAPPS program, you first need to focus your passion on attending to details, that is, on not missing any step in the process.

Learning to think aloud and to monitor your thinking carefully, in a step-by-step manner, will use every bit of your brain power. Our experience with thousands of students is that the extra distractions of important problem situations add more than our brains can handle. Cognitive science has consistently shown that the novice's channel capacity is very limited in comparison with the expert's. This means that learners need to focus on a few things in order to avoid getting lost in the big picture. By getting caught up in the meaning of the problem, you forget to pay attention to careful step-by-step analysis. While you are learning the first steps in TAPPS, it is best to work with simple, unimportant, silly problems.

These kinds of problems can be great fun. When they are solved using TAPPS, there is a great deal of excitement; this comes not from the problem situations but from the experience of watching the human mind at work. The thrill is similar to that in a good detective mystery. We are much less interested in what the solution is than in how the solution is found.

In sports we find a somewhat similar strategy in calisthenics. These are warm-up and training exercises designed to prepare one for playing the real game. Each exercise is simple and on its own rather silly. But practicing these exercises is critical to success on the playing field. The exercises in *Problem Solving and Comprehension* are designed to strengthen certain mental "muscle groups" critical to success in all areas of academic work. Without well-developed skills in these areas, you are bound to drop the ball.

Once you have mastered the exercises in this book, you will want to apply the skills you learned to real-world problem solving. But until these skills are automatic and require little conscious attention, you will find yourself forgetting to work step by step. You may get distracted by emotions, or you may just lose your chain of thought, because there are too many interesting things to keep track of. The only way to guard against these distractions is to practice the basics over and over in as simple a context as possible.

The Demands of Work

While new standards are being formulated for the academic subjects, equally important new criteria are being generated by business and labor. One extremely influential document is *What Work Requires of Schools* (SCANS, 1991), better known as the Secretary's Commission on Achieving Necessary Skills (SCANS) report because it was produced by the U.S. Department of Labor Secretary's Commission on Achieving Necessary Skills. In it a commission made up of industry and labor leaders reports on the skills every high school graduate must have to be competitive in the work place of the 21st century. The report contains the following dramatic conclusions:

> High paying but unskilled jobs are disappearing.
>
> . . . good jobs depend on people who can put knowledge to work. New workers must be creative and responsible problem solvers and have the skills and attitudes on which employers can build. (p. v)
>
> [Those who] cannot learn these skills by the time they leave high school . . . face bleak prospects, dead-end work, interrupted only by periods of un-employment. (p. viii)
>
> SCANS Report, 1991

The specific skills needed are summarized in the chart that follows.

The relevance of *Problem Solving and Comprehension* to the skills enumerated in the SCANS report is underscored by former Secretary of Labor Robert Reich in *The Work of Nations* (1991): "In the vast literature on experimental learning, two works stand out: D. A. Kolb's 'On Management and the Learning Process,' in D. A. Kolb et al. (Eds.), *Organizational Psychology: A Book of Readings* (2nd ed.; Englewood Cliffs, NJ: Prentice Hall, 1974), and A. Whimbey and J. Lockhead (sic), *Problem Solving and Comprehension*."

Problem Solving and Comprehension addresses many of the SCANS competencies and foundation skills. Problem-solving strategies such as those used in problem 9 (p. 61) and problems 6 through 14 (pp. 129–131) provide an important foundation to effective use of "**Resources**—allocating time, money, materials, space and staff." The listener–problem solver dialog used in TAPPS is probably the strongest foundation available on which to build

WORKPLACE KNOW-HOW

The know-how identified by SCANS is made up of five competencies and a three-part foundation of skills and personal qualities that are needed for solid job performance. These include:

COMPETENCIES — effective workers can productively use:

- **Resources** — allocating time, money, materials, space, and staff;

- **Interpersonal Skills** — working on teams, teaching others, serving customers, leading, negotiating, and working well with people from culturally diverse backgrounds;

- **Information** — acquiring and evaluating data, organizing and maintaining files, interpreting and communicating, and using computers to process information;

- **Systems** — understanding social, organizational, and technological systems, monitoring and correcting performance, and designing or improving systems;

- **Technology** — selecting equipment and tools, applying technology to specific tasks, and maintaining and troubleshooting technologies.

THE FOUNDATION — competence requires:

- **Basic Skills** — reading, writing, arithmetic and mathematics, speaking, and listening;

- **Thinking Skills** — thinking creatively, making decisions, solving problems, seeing things in the mind's eye, knowing how to learn, and reasoning;

- **Personal Qualities** — individual responsibility, self-esteem, sociability, self-management, and integrity.

"**Interpersonal Skills**—working on teams, teaching others, serving customers, leading, negotiating, and working well with people from culturally diverse backgrounds." The problems in chapters 4, 9, 10, and 11 all develop important skills for "**Information**—acquiring and evaluating data, organizing and maintaining files, interpreting and communicating, ..."

Problem Solving and Comprehension provides complete coverage of the Foundation Competencies. Working through the entire text is an excellent way to review "**Basic Skills**—reading, writing, arithmetic and mathematics, speaking, and listening." Working through the complete text also establishes a strong foundation in "**Thinking Skills**—thinking creatively, making decisions, solving problems, seeing things in the mind's eye, knowing how to learn, and reasoning." Finally, the text provides a strong foundation for the important "**Personal Qualities**—individual responsibility, self-esteem, sociability, self-management, and integrity." It may not be immediately apparent how the TAPPS process can build a strong basis for these personal qualities. Individual responsibility and self-esteem are qualities that each person has to construct for himself or herself. No amount of inspired lecturing can magically transfer these qualities from teacher to student. In TAPPS, pairs of learners have direct experience in how to be responsible for the accuracy of their own work and in understanding that they cannot always depend on an external expert or teacher for confirmation of success. This understanding is the meaning of individual responsibility and the only valid basis on which to build self esteem.

Preparing for Academic and Workplace Assessment Systems

Terra Nova

The *Terra Nova* (McGraw-Hill, 1997) is an example of the new student assessment systems that are being developed in response to revised national and state academic standards. Among the test's innovations is an extensive Thinking Skills Framework. We have related this framework to the material in *Problem Solving and Comprehension* (PS&C I), its successor *Beyond Problem Solving and Comprehension* (PS&C II; Whimbey & Lochhead, 1984); *The Whimbey Writing Program* (WWP) and *Analytical Writing and Thinking* (AWT); *Developing Mathematical Skills* (DMS; Whimbey & Lochhead, 1981); and *Analytical Reading and Reasoning* (ARR) and its companion *Mastering Reading Through Reasoning* (MRR; Whimbey, 1995). In the following table, we show where each of these books offers instruction and practice exercises for each skill in the framework. In many cases a problem will involve more than one thinking skill and thus its placement in the table may seem somewhat arbitrary. Most of the skills appear in several parts of the *Terra Nova*, including both the mathematics and the English language sections. It is wise, therefore, to practice them in at least these two contexts.

Alignment of Terra Nova Thinking Skills With Whimbey Thinking Program

Terra Nova Thinking Skills	Problem Solving and Comprehension
Gather Information	
Observe—direct observation as well as matching of visual symbols and shapes.	Observation problems involving overlapping shapes, Venn diagrams and alpha-numeric information are found on pages 81 to 118, PS&C I. (See also: pp. 19–44 and 145–214 in PS&C II, pp. 1–35 WWP and pp. 4–6, 36–37 AWT, all of DMS but especially chap 2.)
Recall—recognizing or performing learned routines and elaborating elements of a complex concept.	Recall is important throughout DMS especially in chapter 1.
Question—formulating questions to obtain needed information.	Questions for gathering information are employed throughout the worked solutions in PS&C I&II as well as in WWP, AWT, DMS.
Organize Information	
Represent—using different forms to structure information such as graphs, charts, maps, etc.	Representation problems involving verbal reasoning are on pages 43 to 77, problems involving sequencing and hypothetical thinking on pages 223 to 239, diagramming mathematical relations pages 244 to 312 in PS&C I. (See also: pp. 1–35 WWP; pp. 50–66 MRR and chapter 10 DMS.)
Compare—identifying similarities and contrasting by identifying differences.	Comparison problems involving verbal and numerical analogies are on pages 143 to 194 PS&C I. (See also pp. 19–44 PS&C II, pp. 151–180 WWP; pp. 99–126 MRR and chapter 12 DMS.)
Classify—identifying examples of a category.	Classification problems involving Venn diagrams are on pages 87 to 104 in PS&C I. (See also: pp. 69–98 WWP and all of DMS for example pp. 119–120.)
Order—producing a scheme or criterion for sequencing, as well as ordering information according to a pre-established scheme.	Ordering problems involving sequencing of trends and patterns are on pages 195–239 PS&C I. (See also: pp. 273–326 PS&C II, pp. 37–63 WWP, pp. 69–84 and 143–156 MRR; pp. 20–24 AWT and all of DMS.)

(Continued)

Terra Nova Thinking Skills	Problem Solving and Comprehension
Analyze Information	
Identify Attributes and Components—finding and labeling the pieces of the whole.	Identifying components appears throughout DMS (e.g. pp. 77–80).
Determine Accuracy and Adequacy—measuring or estimating accuracy.	Determining accuracy appears throughout DMS (e.g. chapter 13, section 5).
Recognize Relationships and Patterns—making causal or hierarchical connections, determining rules of relationships and patterns.	Problems involving the recognition of relationships inherent in analogies are on pages 143 to 239 PS&C I. (See also: pp. 19–44 in PS&C II, pp. 11–19, 25–28, 38–44, 50–62, 78–88, 100–110, 115–119, 129–140, 148–152, 156–191, 201–204 AWT.) Recognizing relationships is a particularly important part of chapter 12 of DMS.
Identify Central Element—identifying the central element, theme or main idea.	Problems involving identification of central element are on pages 131 to 136 WWP and pages 177 to 190 MRR.
Generate Ideas	
Infer—extending or expanding available information.	Inferential problems involving language translation are on pages 119 to 137 PS&C I. (See also: pp. 251–271 and 343–356 PS&C II, pp. 207–437 AWT.)

Predict—forecast future events or consequences.

Prediction problems involving alpha-numeric trends and patterns are on pages 195–221 PS&C I. (See also: pp. 273–326 PS&C II.)

Restructure—using analogies, making hypotheses, transferring to new situations.

Restructuring problems involving analogies are found on pages 143 to 194 PS&C I. Restructuring is the central tool in the WWP, numerous exercises are found on pages 1 to 203 in WWP and throughout AWT, ARR, and MRR.

Synthesize Elements

Summarize—combine key elements in a concise manner.

Foundation exercises for summarizing are found in chapter 1 of WWP. See also chapter 1 of *Analyze Organize Write.*

Integrate—form a meaningful whole that fits together.

Problems involving the integration of data from graphs and tables are on pages 145 to 214 of PS&C II.

Evaluate Outcomes

Establish Criteria—setting standards for evaluating quality or adequacy.

Problems involving the establishing of criteria appear on pages 111 to 114, 153 to 155 AWT.

Verify—judging outcomes by comparison to established criteria.

Comparison to criteria is an important component of the listener's role in PS&C I&II.

Work Keys

The American College Testing service (ACT, 1995) has developed a battery of tests designed to measure essential job related skills. The Work Keys assessment package contains eight different tests each designed to measure a wide range of competencies. Tests are available in the following areas: Applied Mathematics, Applied Technology, Writing, Listening, Locating Information, Reading for Information, Teamwork, Observation.

The tests are scored on a four-level scale. The lowest level (level 3) covers skills usually learned in high school, whereas the highest levels, 6 and 7, are typical of those developed in advanced graduate degree programs. No one is expected to score high in all eight areas. ACT has established score profiles to fit a large number of different occupations. Many industries have found that the Work Keys test battery accurately measures skills that are relevant to their needs, and for this reason the test is rapidly gaining acceptance in the hiring selection process. But the test is also an excellent tool for designing a program of study. The Work Keys system is designed so that students can compare their Work Keys profile to the profile of any desired career. From this they can tell immediately which areas of competence they must develop further and by how much.

Problem Solving and Comprehension can be a useful part of any program designed to establish high school (level 3 or 4) preparation in three of the eight tests: applied mathematics, locating information, and reading for information. Similarly, *Analytical Thinking and Writing* provides a high school level preparation for the Writing test. *Beyond Problem Solving and Comprehension* covers material that should be adequate for graduate school performance (level 7) in applied Math. We believe that a significant amount of experience with TAPPS should improve scores on the listening, observation, and teamwork tests, but at present cannot quantify that effect.

Alignment of Work Keys and Whimbey Thinking Program

Work Keys	Problem Solving and Comprehension
Applied Mathematics	Preparation for level 3 or 4 is available in chapters 4, 9, 10, and 11 of PS&C I. A level 7 preparation is available, working all problems in PS&C II.
Locating Information	Preparation for level 3 or 4 is available in chapters 10 and 11 of PS&C I and in chapter 4 of PS&C II.
Reading for Information	Preparation for level 3 or 4 is available in chapters 4, 5, 8, 10, and 11 of PS&C I. Additional important exercises are found in WWP, AWR, MRR, and ARR.
Listening Observation Teamwork	These three tests require preparation beyond that provided in PS&C. They all benefit, however, from extensive practice with the Thinking Aloud Pair Problem Solving strategy.
Applied Technology	This test requires extensive hands-on experience with tools and with basic elementary physics concepts. Chapters 2 and 7 in PS&C II may assist in providing additional mental flexibility useful in some parts of this test.

XIV. HOW TO USE PAIR PROBLEM SOLVING

In this book, we have used pair problem solving to develop the basic analytical reasoning skills essential for success on standardized tests and throughout school. In a sequel, *Beyond Problem Solving and Comprehension* (Whimbey & Lochhead, 1984), we provide a thorough preparation for the quantitative sections of the SAT, as well as for the GRE and the professional examinations. But pair problem solving has a much wider array of applications. In this chapter we consider how teachers, students, parents, and managers can use pair problem solving in many of their normal activities.

Teachers

Pair problem solving can be a lively alternative to modes of teaching you normally employ. Only in rare circumstances is it appropriate as the primary method of instruction, but it is extremely useful whenever there is a need to reach a deeper understanding of some form of analysis. A good time for pair problem solving is whenever students are having more difficulty than you think they should. It might be when you first introduce word problems involving percentage calculations or when you assign the first Russian novel in a literature class. Not only will pair problem solving encourage students to think carefully about what they are doing, it will also provide you with an opportunity to listen in and possibly discover the cause of the most serious problems.

All you need to conduct a pair problem-solving class is a few short problems and a brief statement of the rules. The first time your class is introduced to pair problem solving it is best to keep the problems easy. This allows students to concentrate on the talking–listening process and not get too caught up in the issues of reaching a correct solution. We recommend that you use problems from an appropriate section of *Problem Solving and Comprehension*. These problems have been proven effective starters with groups ranging from elementary school children to college professors. Once your class is comfortable with pair problem solving you can use it in a wide variety of situations, and you may find it useful to modify the rules to encourage many different kinds of group work. We consider a few of the options in the sections here.

Triads and Other Options

Many different group structures can be built out of the practice and experience gained in pair problem solving. One of the most commonly used approaches is the triad in which the third member of the group acts as an observer–recorder or, alternatively, a referee. This person's function is to watch the other two and comment on how well they are staying in their roles. Teachers who use pair problem solving at the elementary level often find that the third member is essential in order to keep the problem solver and listener aware of their own actions. For some children, it is only through the experience of watching other listeners that they can learn to control their own listening behavior. (Problems appropriate for elementary school can be found in *Thinking Through Math Word Problems* by Whimbey, Lochhead, & Potter, 1990.) There is no limit to the number of different group combinations and roles that can be generated. The design that is best for you and your students is something you must find for yourself. As long as students are involved with their work and learning new ways of thinking the goals of pair problem solving are being met.

Mathematics and Science

Problems form a natural part of most math and science courses. Pair problem solving works best with problems involving more than straight calculation, such as word problems presenting situations that must be analyzed and reformulated before beginning calculations. Pure calculation, whether arithmetic or algebraic, rarely provide room for discussion. This is because most students perform calculations on automatic; they are largely unaware of the choices made in deciding what step to do next.

Classic end-of-chapter word problems are not the only option. If students are having difficulty reading their text, ask the problem solver to paraphrase a sentence or paragraph while the listener probes to find out how the translation is being made. The problem solver could be asked to take a position on some controversial application of science and to defend it (e.g., should rabbits be used in research?). Problems from old SAT or Regents exams might be used if improved performance on these tests is a goal of your course. With multiple choice tests it is sometimes possible to find which distractor items are most commonly selected by the students you teach. If you have such information you might ask the problem solver to explain a line of reasoning that could produce the most popular incorrect answers. Alternatively the problem-solving pair could take turns defining a line of reasoning for each possible answer in sequence and then decide which of all the given answers represents the best choice and why.

English

English teachers are sometimes at a loss for short problems. Texts such as *Analyze, Organize, Write* (Whimbey & Jenkins, 1987), *Analytical Writing and Thinking* (Linden & Whimbey, 1990a), and *Analytical Reading and Reasoning* (Whimbey, 1989), provide a wealth of short problems. Other appropriate tasks include:

Sentence ordering: Students are given a set of jumbled sentences and asked to order them to form a coherent paragraph.

Text interpretation: The problem solver is asked to give the meaning of a sentence, paragraph, or stanza.

Error correction: The problem solver is given a text that has some number of errors that must be found.

Additional suggestions may be found in *Why Johnny Can't Write* (Linden & Whimbey, 1990b).

Social Studies

Many of the techniques described in the two previous sections can be used in the social disciplines: paraphrasing paragraphs, taking and defending a position, chronologically or logically connecting a series of events. Standardized tests and distractor items can also be analyzed. Discussion and debate are critical aspects of the social sciences. Pair problem solving is an excellent preparation for participation in larger group discussions; it increases the precision of the speakers and the attention and critical astuteness of the listeners.

Languages

The techniques described for English also apply to foreign language instruction. In addition, the following extension may prove useful. Pair 1 translates a sentence from English to French and gives the translation to Pair 2. The second pair translates the French back to English. Finally all four students get together to compare the original English with the derived English; if the meaning of these two sentences is incompatible, the group then must decide where the mistranslation occurred.

Adjusting to the Pace

Most teachers find their first experiences with pair problem solving a little disquieting. The students are busy; the room is noisy but you the teacher may not be sure what to do. You can sit with a group and listen in, but often this results in the pair looking to you for guidance rather than getting on with their task. If you keep quiet and out of the way you may feel that you are not doing your job, or to put it another way you may feel ignored and unimportant. Pair problem solving does require that you look on your job as a teacher in a new light. It is the students who are the workers; you are a manager and as long as the students are working effectively you *are* doing your job. Often there will be more than enough questions to keep you busy but when there aren't, enjoy the break, you deserve it. For more insight into this view of teaching read *Control Theory in the Classroom* (Glasser, 1986).

Students

Pair problem solving is an excellent study tool. Learning is more effective and homework more enjoyable when you do it with other students. Yet when two or more students get together to study they often find other things to do and may not know how to work well as a team. Pair problem solving is a good way to develop meaningful cooperation. Once you have learned to be a good listener and to ask tough questions you can always make sure that the problem solver does not get away with a solution that may sound good but that does not really make sense. Study groups of up to five students can operate with one student solving a problem while all of the others ask questions. If the problem solver gets stuck another student may be able to take over.

Pair problem solving can also be useful when you must study alone. We know of one physicist who used to study for exams by writing out a detailed solution to a problem (acting the role of problem solver) and then attacking the solution (acting out the role of listener). The listener role can also be useful when you read. Ask the author how he/she comes to his conclusions or what evidence he/she has for her views. Of course the authors cannot answer back so you will have to give them some help yourself.

Parents

Instead of telling your children how to do their algebra, try working with them as a listener. That way you can help even when you do not understand the material yourself (and if you are a good listener your kids may never find out that you are in over your head!). Pair problem solving can do a great deal more than improve learning; it can advance interpersonal understanding. Once, in the end-of-the-year evaluations of a math course that used pair problem solving, a student reported that the course had taught him to get along better with his mother. What he probably meant by this was that he had learned to listen to people who had different ideas from his own and that he now could appreciate their reasoning. Standard tutoring or lecturing is a one way process. It is usually pretty frustrating to all concerned and tends to drive people apart. Pair problem solving helps people understand each other and brings them closer together.

Pair Problem Solving in the Workplace

Today cooperation is replacing competition in more and more work situations. Yet few of us have any training in cooperative thinking or group problem solving. Pair problem solving is an excellent system for building skills for team thinking, creativity, trouble shooting, and design. Often when a group of people meet to discuss an issue, each individual strives to show off his or her own competence or cut down other people's ideas. To counter these tendencies a technique known as brainstorming forbids criticism. But this does not really solve the problem, because criticism is essential to building an effective solution. Pair problem solving encourages constant criticism without degenerating into personal bickering.

Most people, including highly talented people, have very little conscious awareness of how they produce creative new ideas or how they reach decisions. When you have little understanding of how you think yourself, the conclusions reached by others can be completely baffling. In the highly charged, competitive environment of the corporate rat race it is easy to see other people's ideas in a bad light. Pair problem solving develops both an understanding of your own reasoning processes and an appreciation of those of other people. Furthermore it shows you how, working with other people, you can refine ideas and problem solutions so that the end result is better than any single contribution. This experience and the experiences of sharing your thought processes create a feeling of intimacy and trust. It establishes the base for a group to move from bickering to brilliance.

APPENDIX I. ANSWER KEY

Chapter I. Test Your Mind
Whimbey Analytical Skills Inventory (WASI)

1. c	20. c
2. c	21. c
3. a	22. d
4. c	23. d
5. d	24. a
6. c	25. Q, Q, G
7. a	26. d
8. O, N	27. d
9. d	28. b
10. c	29. b
11. d	30. d
12. d	31. d
13. c	32. b
14. 87, 83	33. c
15. e	34. stop
16. e	35. c
17. d	36. b
18. pardøn	37. c
19. c	38. b

Chapter IV. Verbal Reasoning Problems
Additional Problems

1. Sally is taller.

2. John is fastest; Harvey is slowest.

3. Fred is tallest; Hal is second tallest.

4. Gladys is heaviest; Violet is lightest.

5. more hatred

    ├ Frankenstein
    ├ Mummy
    ├ Wolfman
    ├ Dracula

    less hatred

6. more
    + Instruction
    + Operation, Maintenance, and Auxiliary Agencies
    + Capital Outlay
    + Interest
    + General Control
   less

7. deeper
    + Superior
    + Michigan
    + Ontario
    + Huron
    + Erie
   shallower

8. $570.00

9.

	Cotton	Wool	Synthetic	Total
Pat	3	4	3	10
Joan	8	3	1	12
Mary	4	3	1	8
Total	15	10	5	30

Joan has 12 dresses.

10. 4

11.

	First Quarter	Second Quarter	Third Quarter	Fourth Quarter	Total
Acme	23	7	4	23	57
B&S	0	50	0	25	75
Arco	0	0	75	0	75
Total	23	57	79	48	207

A total of 57 houses was sold in the second quarter.

12. Nancy

13. Judy—Housewife; Celia—Math Teacher; Betty—Truck Driver

14. Rose—Saleswoman; Hannah—Shipping Clerk; Geraldine—Cashier; Mary Jo—Stockgirl

15. West

16. Northwest

17. 5 hours and 45 minutes

18. East-West

19. Parallel

20. Perpendicular

21.

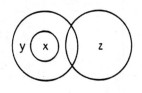

22.

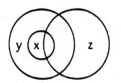

23.

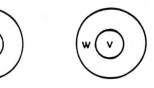

24.

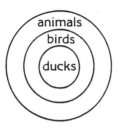

25.

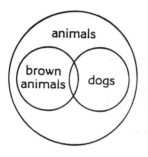

26.

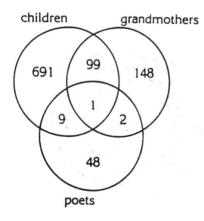

Total Homes = 998

27.

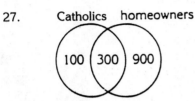

Catholics homeowners

Total votes = 1300

28. *a.*   no
    b.   no

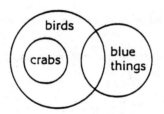

29. *a.*   no
    b.   yes

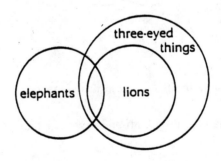

30. *a.* no
    b. yes

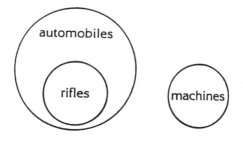

31. *a.* No. The question mark shows we don't know whether some usable things are paper.

    b. Yes. The ✓ shows that some paper is white and therefore not usable.

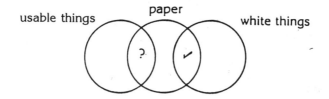

32. fireplace

33. (Otherwise,) circle the first word in this sentence.

34. If deleting the first, third, fifth and seventh letters . . .

35. Jonathan

36. sanctuary

37. *8 9 7 5 5* ③ *9 9 2 4 6*

38. 9 8 7 6 5 4 3 2 1. Take the difference between the first number and the sixth number. Write the difference here <u>5</u>. Now take the difference between the fifth number and the seventh number. Write it here <u>2</u>. Finally, take the difference between these two differences and write it here <u>3</u>.

39. *8②7 5 6 4 5 3 4.*

40. *c. 10*

41. gi ra

42. *c. ba si*

43. 1934 Cardinals beat Tigers (Dean)
    1942 Cardinals beat Yankees
    1943 Yankees beat Cardinals
    1944 Cardinals beat Browns (aka Orioles)
    1946 Cardinals beat Red Sox (Slaughter)
    1964 Cardinals beat Yankees
    1967 Cardinals beat Red Sox
    1968 Tigers beat Cardinals (Lolich)
    1982 Cardinals beat Brewers

Chapter VI. Analogies
Analogy Problems

1. a		13. b
2. c		14. b
3. b		15. c
4. c		16. b
5. b		17. c
6. c		18. b
7. b		19. a
8. c		20. c
9. a		21. a
10. a		22. b
11. b		23. a
12. a		24. b

Chapter VII. Writing Relationship Sentences
Samples of Acceptable Relationship Sentences for Relationship Problems

1. _____ is the opposite of _____.

2. _____ are kept in a _____.

3. A _____ was used before a(n) _____, but for the same purpose.

4. A _____ controls the action of a(n) _____.

5. A(n) _____ gives birth to a _____.

6. _____ energizes a _____.

7. An _____ needs _____.

8. The _____ provide(s) nutrition for a(n) _____.

9. The _____ is at the end of the limb which is attached to the body by the _____.

10. A _____ is a type of _____.

11. A _____ is given by a _____.

12. A _____ hunts a _____.

13. _____ is three times _____.

14. _____ is 30 less than _____.

15. _____ is ⅓ of _____.

16. _____ is 30 more than _____.

17. _____ is 2½ times _____.

18. (A) _____ are at the base of a _____.

19. The _____ revolves around the _____.

20. _____ travel together in a _____.

21. A _____ is used to produce _____.

22. _____ is a mild form of _____.

23. _____ is the extreme of _____.

24. The purpose of a(n) _____ is to counter _____.

25. A _____ is a three-dimensional _____.

26. A _____ is a signal before a _____.

27. A(n) _____ is the outline of a _____.

28. _____ can be used to _____.

29. A _____ extends into the _____.

30. A(n) _____ is the origin of a(n) _____.

31. A _____ may be the light source of a _____.

32. _____ is an inactive state of a(n) _____.

33. _____ means _____.

Chapter VIII. How to Form Analogies

Section	Answer	Relationship Sentence
5	c	_____ is ⅓ of _____.
6	d	A _____ is run by a _____.
7	c	A(n) _____ is a collection of _____.
10	c	_____ is in the form of a _____.
13	d	_____ is the natural covering of a _____.
14	c	A _____ is part human and part _____.

Chapter VIII. Analogy Problems

	Answer	Relationship Sentence
1.	b	A _____ stands on a _____.
2.	c	A _____ is used for hitting in _____.
3.	d	(A) _____ is produced at a _____.
4.	c	A _____ is a unit of _____.
5.	d	_____ is three months before _____.
6.	c	_____ make up a(n) _____.
7.	d	_____ is destructive to _____.
8.	d	_____ is the meat obtained from _____.
9.	d	A _____ extends from the _____.
10.	b	A _____ is part of a(n) _____.
11.	a	A _____ produces _____.
12.	c	The product of a _____ is a _____.
13.	c	A _____ is used to measure _____.
14.	d	_____ is the reward of _____.
15.	b	A _____ sells high _____ food.
16.	c	A _____ fights _____.
17.	c	_____ and _____ sound the same.
18.	c	A _____ may be made of _____.
19.	a	One part of a _____ is a _____.

20.	b	_____ stimulates the growth of _____.
21.	a	A _____ is bigger than but similar to a _____.
22.	a	A(n) _____ may give rise to a(n) _____.
23.	b	A(n) _____ is (can be) surrounded by (the) _____.
24.	b	_____ is a _____.

Chapter IX. Analysis of Trends and Patterns
Problems in Identifying Patterns

1. *42 47 50*

   Pattern description: Alternately add 5 and 3.

   or

   Each number is 8 more than two numbers before it.

2. *A B B*

   Pattern description: A single A alternates with alternately one or two *B*s.

3. *g*

   Pattern description: Numbers running backwards alternate with letters that go up the alphabet skipping a letter each time.

4. *17 20 19*

   Pattern description: Alternately add 3 and subtract 1.

   or

   Each number is 2 more than two numbers before it.

5. *J I L*

   Pattern description: Go down one letter, then up three letters, repeated.

   or

   Letters go up the alphabet in sets of two, with the two letters within each set in reverse order.

6. *Q L Q*

   Pattern description: Qs alternate with *L*s. With the Qs there are alternately 2 or 4. With the *L*s there are alternately 1 or 3.

7. *7 4 2*

   Pattern description: Alternately subtract 3 and subtract 2.

                                                    or

                         Each new number is 5 less than two numbers before it.

8. *W E V*

   Pattern description: Letters going up the alphabet alternate with letters going down the alphabet.

9. *18 20 15*

   Pattern description: Alternately subtract 5 and add 2.

                                                    or

                         Each new number is 3 less than two numbers before it.

10. *121212 1212121*

   Pattern description: Each set becomes longer by alternately adding 1 or 2.

11. *43 52 62*

   Pattern description: Each time add 1 more than was previously added.

12. *129 126 119*

   Pattern description: Subtract 3, subtract 7, add 4, then repeat.

                                                    or

                         Each number is 6 less than three numbers before it.

13. *T I R*

   Pattern description: There are two alternating series of letters. One series skips a letter going up the alphabet. The other series skips a letter coming down the alphabet.

14. *P 5 M*

   Pattern description: The letters *J, P,* and *M* alternate with the numbers 1, 3, 5, and 8.

15. *5 1 2 C P*

    Pattern description: Each letter is followed by a number showing its po-
    sition in the alphabet.

16. *320 640 1280*

    Pattern description: Each new number is twice the previous number.

17. *38H 46F*

    Pattern description: Numbers alternate with letters. Each new number is
    obtained by adding 1 more than was added in getting
    the previous number. The letters run backwards in
    the alphabet, each time skipping a letter.

18. *85 75 64*

    Pattern description: Each new number is obtained by subtracting 1 more
    than was subtracted in getting the previous number.

19. *B 2 A B*

    Pattern description: Groups of letters alternate with groups of numbers.
    The letters are *A B C B A*. The numbers are *1 2 3
    2 1*.

20. *M M 13 B M*

    Pattern description: Groups of letters alternate with groups of numbers.
    The letters are *B M N M B*. The numbers are *2 13
    14 13 2*.

21. *486 1458*

    Pattern description: Each new number is three times the previous num-
    ber.

22. *3F F4 3E G2*

    Pattern description: Each entry consists of a letter and a number and
    begins alternately with one or the other. The numbers
    are *2 3 4 3 2 3 4 3 2 3* etc. The letters start with *A*
    and go up one letter, repeat that letter, then go down
    one letter. Next jump up two letters, go up one letter,
    repeat that letter, go down one letter. Next jump up
    two letters, etc.

23. *K P P*

Pattern description: Each letter is repeated once; then the next letter is obtained by going up the alphabet one more letter than the last time.

24. *I K I*

Pattern description: Up 2 letters, up 2 letters, down 2 letters, repeated.

25. *2 1 ½ ¼*

Pattern description: Each new number is one-half the previous number.

26. *11 K 11 1 A A*

Pattern description: Sets of numbers alternate with sets of letters. The numbers are *1 11 20 11 1*. The letters are *A K T K A*.

27. *ACEG GACE*

Pattern description: Starting with the letters *ACEG*, each successive entry has the letter from the back of the previous entry moved to the front.

28. *000X0X0 0000X0X*

Pattern description: In each entry the *X*s are one position to the right compared to the previous entry.

29. *34 33 66*

Pattern description: Alternately multiply by 2 and subtract 1.

30. *28 21 13*

Pattern description: Starting with the number 49, first 1 is subtracted, then 2 is subtracted, then 3 is subtracted, and in each case 1 more is subtracted than was subtracted last.

31. *4 13 3*

Pattern description: Starting with 8, first 1 is added, then 2 is subtracted, then 3 is added, and this pattern of alternately adding and subtracting 1 more number is continued.

32. *38 76 78*

Pattern description: Alternately add 2 and multiply by 2.

33. *24FP 26GV*

Pattern description: Each entry has a number and two letters. The numbers are obtained by alternately adding 2 and 5. The first letter in each entry is one letter higher in the alphabet than the first letter in the previous entry. The second letter in each entry is obtained by skipping one more letter than was skipped in getting the second letter of the previous entry.

34. *T W V*

Pattern description: Up 3 letters, down 1 letter, up 2 letters, repeated.

35. *720 40,320*

Pattern description: Each entry is multiplied by 1 more than the previous entry was multiplied by.

36. *17 21*

Pattern description: The third number in each set is the sum of the first two numbers.

37. *9 10 21*

Pattern description: The third number in each set is the sum of the first two numbers.

38. *34 55 89*

Pattern description: Each number is the sum of the two previous numbers.

39. *68 125 230*

Pattern description: Each number is the sum of the three previous numbers.

40. *8700 8600 9600*

Pattern description: Alternately add 1000 and subtract 100.

41. *31 36 38*

Pattern description: Add 5, add 2, subtract 1, then repeat.

42. *70 80 87*

    Pattern description: Add 10, add 7, add 5, then repeat.

43. *18 19 38*

    Pattern description: Subtract 4, add 1, multiply by 2, then repeat.

44. g g

    Pattern Description: Single letters alternate with double letters. The single letters simply go up the alphabet. The double letters go up the alphabet but skip a letter each time.

45. f l

    Pattern Description: Three independent series of letters alternate. The first series begins with c and simply goes up the alphabet: c d e f. The second series begins with i and simply goes up the alphabet: i j k l.

46. g p

    Pattern Description: Three series of letters alternate. The first series begins with d and goes up the alphabet. The second series begins with g and skips two letters each time as it goes up the alphabet.

47. l e

    Pattern Description: Three series of letters alternate. The first series begins with u and goes backwards through the alphabet. The second series begins with n and goes backwards through the alphabet.

Chapter X. Deductive and Hypothetical Thinking
Days of the Week Problems

Part I.

    1. Monday
    2. Sunday
    3. a. Friday
       b. Monday

Part II.

    1. Sunday
    2. Thursday
    3. a. Saturday
       b. Tuesday

Part III.

1. Sunday
2. Friday
3. Sunday
4. Thursday

Part IV.

1. Sunday
2. Tuesday
3. Saturday
4. Thursday
5. Wednesday
6. Monday
7. a. Tuesday
8. Sunday

Part V.

1. d. Wednesday
2. d. Thursday
3. d. Monday
   e. Sunday
4. d. Monday
   e. Tuesday
   f. Wednesday

Part VI.

1. g. Thursday
2. g. Tuesday
3. Sunday
4. Sunday
5. Wednesday
6. Wednesday

Part VII.

1. n
2. second
3. 20th
4. 13
5. 3 days
6. d.
7. Friday
8. Saturday

9. Sunday
10. Wednesday

Extra Practice Problems

1. Friday
2. Tuesday
3. Saturday
4. Wednesday
5. Thursday
6. $438
7. $300
8. $11/60$

Chapter XI. Solving Mathematical Word Problems
Additional Problems

1. 450 mi
2. 25 ft
3. *a.* 5
   b. 2½
   c. 25
   d. 205
4. 27
5. 44 in
6. 60 in
7. 12½ min
8. $170.00
9. $60.00
10. $50.00
11. $225.00
12. $170.00
13. 12
14. 4
15. Heaviest—Bill
    Lightest—Al
16. 8
17. 13
18. *a.* 16
    b. 2
19. 13
20. 200 ft
21. 30 ft
22. 90 mi

23. even
24. odd
25. odd
26. either
27. even
28. either
29. 10
30. *a.* .3 sq mi
    b. 2.2 mi
31. *a.* 2.25 sq mi
    b. 6 mi
32. 60 mi
33. .3 mi
34. 12/18 or 2/3
35. 9/36 or 1/4
36. .088
37. *a.* $2800.00
    b. $1200.00
38. *a.* $120.00
    b. $420.00
39. $1750.00
40. C and D
41. *a.* V and W
    b. X and Y
42. *a.* a
    b. b
43. *a.* 1/10
    b. 1/30
    c. 5
    d. 1/5
    e. 1
    f. $1/4^2$
44. *a.* less
    b. less
    c. $100.00
45. *a.* 6
    b. 216 sq in
46. *a.* 12
    b. 288 sq in
47. *a.* 24
    b. 360
48. $78.00
49. 30
50. 624
51. $238

52. *a.*

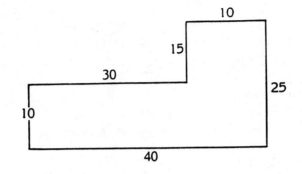

    b. 130 mi

53. 550 sq mi
54. a.

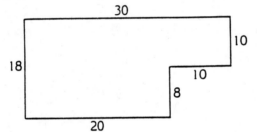

    b. 96 mi

55. 460 sq mi
56. $125.00
57. $160.00
58. $380.00
59. $2420.00
60. (2, 2) (4, −4)
    distance = $\sqrt{40}$ = 6.32
61. 9
62. −8
63. −5

64. $\dfrac{d^2}{3}$

65. x

Chapter XII. The Post-WASI Test

1. C
2. C
3. south
4. B
5. D
6. A
7. sa
8. N K
9. accountant
10. 160
11. B
12. C
13. B
14. 10, 5, 1
15. B
16. B
17. $320
18. B
19. D

20. DI©TION
21. B
22. C
23. 8
24. C
25. sQ, uN, wO
26. D
27. D
28. B
29. C
30. C
31. C
32. B
33. D
34. Tuesday
35. C
36. 17
37. C
38. C

APPENDIX II. COMPUTE YOUR OWN IQ

You can use the following table to approximate your IQ from your WASI score. Your IQ can vary, depending upon your health and psychological condition. So don't regard your computed IQ as a fixed quantity. If you scored 35 or more on the WASI you should have no trouble with advanced high school and college work, assuming you are willing to devote the necessary time and effort to it. But if you scored below 35, the exercises in this book will be extremely useful in improving your academic aptitude and computed IQ.

Students below age 17 are expected to score lower on the WASI. For students between 14–16, the IQ can be approximated by using the appropriate table.

The IQ of students below 14 cannot be accurately estimated from the WASI, but the exercises in the book can still be used to improve their analytical reasoning skills.

A full explanation of the history and limitations of IQ measurement can be found in *Intelligence Can Be Taught* by Arthur Whimbey.

Adult: 17 and Older		WASI Scores for Younger Age Groups		
WASI Score	IQ Score	Age 16	Age 15	Age 14
Over 35 →	Over 125 ←	Over 34	Over 33	Over 32
33–35	122–125	32–34	31–33	30–32
31–32	119–121	30–31	29–30	28–29
29–30	116–118	28–29	27–28	26–27
27–28	113–115	26–27	25–26	24–25
25—26	110–112	24–25	23–24	22–23
23–24	107–109	22–23	21–22	20–21
21–22	104–106	20–21	19–20	18–19
19–20	101–103	18–19	17–18	16–17
17–18	98–100	16–17	15–16	14–15
15–16	95–97	14–15	13–14	12–13
Below 15	Below 95	Below 14	Below 13	Below 12

REFERENCES

American College Testing Service (1995). *Work Keys Test Description.* Iowa City, IA: ACT Publications.

Boyer Commission (1998). *Reinventing undergraduate education.* Stony Brook, NY: Author.

Brown, A. L., & Palincsar, A. S. (1989). Guided cooperative learning and individual knowledge acquisition. L. Resnick (Ed.), *Knowing, learning, and instruction: Essays in honor of Robert Glaser.* Hillsdale, NJ: Lawrence Erlbaum Associates.

Clay, M. (1985). *The early detection of reading difficulties* (3rd. ed.). Aukland, New Zealand: Heiniman Education Books.

Clay, M. (1991). *Reading recovery: A Guidebook for teachers in training.* Aukland, New Zealand: Heiniman Education Books.

Clay, M. (1993). *Becoming literate: The construction of inner control.* Aukland, New Zealand: Heiniman Education Books.

Glasser, W. (1986). *Control theory in the classroom.* New York: Harper & Row.

Linden, M. J., & Whimbey, A. (1990a). *Analytical writing and thinking.* Hillsdale, NJ: Lawrence Erlbaum Associates.

Linden, M. J., & Whimbey, A. (1990b). *Why Johnny can't write.* Hillsdale, NJ: Lawrence Erlbaum Associates.

National Council of Teachers of Mathematics. (1989). *Curriculum and evaluation standards for school mathematics.* Reston, VA: Author.

NRC. (1996). *National Science Education Standards.* Washington, DC: National Academy Press.

Reich, R. B. (1991). *The work of nations: Preparing ourselves for 21st-century capitalism,* New York: Alfred A. Knopf.

Resnick, L. B. (1987). Learning in school and out. *Educational Researcher, 16*(9), 13–20.

Secretary's Commission on Achieving Necessary Skills (1991). *What work requires of schools.* Washington, DC: Dept. of Labor.

Teacher's Guide to Terra Nova. (1997). Monterey, CA: CTB/McGraw-Hill.

Whimbey, A. (1989). *Analytical reading and reasoning* (2nd ed.). Cary, NC: Innovative Sciences.

Whimbey, A. (1995). *Mastering reading through reasoning.* Cary, NC: Innovative Sciences.

Whimbey, A., & Blanton, E. L. (1995). *The Whimbey Writing Program: How to analyze, organize, and write effectively.* Mahwah, NJ: LEARNING, Inc.

Whimbey, A., & Jenkins, E. L. (1987). *Analyze organize write.* Hillsdale, NJ: Lawrence Erlbaum Associates.

Whimbey, A., Johnson, M. H., Williams, E., Sr., & Linden, M. J. (1993). *Blueprint for educational change.* Atlanta, GA: The Right Combination.

Whimbey, A., & Lochhead, J. (1981). *Developing mathematical skills.* New York: McGraw-Hill.

Whimbey, A., & Lochhead, J. (1984). *Beyond problem solving and comprehension.* Hillsdale, NJ: Lawrence Erlbaum Associates.

Whimbey, A., Lochhead, J., & Potter, P. (1990). *Thinking through math word problems.* Hillsdale, NJ: Lawrence Erlbaum Associates.

Other books of related interest ...

THINKING THROUGH MATH WORD PROBLEMS
Strategies for Intermediate Elementary School Students
Arthur Whimbey, Jack Lochhead, and Paula B. Potter
This innovative text teaches elementary school students the techniques of critical thinking and problem solving and applies those methods to mathematical word problems.
0-8058-0603-2 (paper) / 1990 / 152pp.
0-8058-0912-0 (Teacher's Manual)

WHY JOHNNY CAN'T WRITE
How To Improve Writing Skills
Myra J. Linden and Arthur Whimbey
Using the sentence combining method for teaching writing, the authors present a rationale for re-thinking and re-tooling the English classroom and consequently making the entire educational system more effective.
8-8058-0852-3 (cloth) / 1990 / 136pp.
8-8058-0853-1 (paper)

ANALYTIC WRITING AND THINKING
Facing the Tests
Myra J. Linden and Arthur Whimbey
Designed to enhance the thinking and writing skills that students need for both academic and occupational success, this textbook prepares students for the verbal portions of the SAT, PSAT, ACT, GED, and CRE.
0-8058-0648-2 (cloth) / 1990 / 464pp.
0-8058-0908-2 (paper)
0-8058-0932-5 (Teacher's Manual)

ANALYZE, ORGANIZE, WRITE
Revised Edition
Arthur Whimbey and Elizabeth Lynn Jenkins
This book offers students a method for understanding and mastering the rhetorical patterns that comprise expository writing via the arrangement of jumbled sentences into logical order.
0-8058-0082-4 (paper) / 1987 / 225pp.
0-8058-0244-4 (Instructor's Manual)

For additional information about these books, including special prices...
Call toll-free: 1-800-9-BOOKS-9
9am to 5pm EST only.

Lawrence Erlbaum Associates, Inc.
10 Industrial Avenue
Mahwah, New Jersey 07430-2262
201/236-9500
FAX 201/236-0072